Steroids and Other
Performance-Enhancing Drugs

JUNIOR DRUG AWARENESS

Alcohol

Amphetamines and
Other Stimulants

Cocaine and Crack

Diet Pills

Ecstasy and Other Club Drugs

Heroin

How to Say No to Drugs

Inhalants and Solvents

Marijuana

Nicotine

Over-the-Counter Drugs

Prozac and Other
Antidepressants

Steroids and Other
Performance-Enhancing
Drugs

Vicodin, OxyContin, and
Other Pain Relievers

JUNIOR DRUG AWARENESS

Steroids and Other Performance-Enhancing Drugs

Krista West

CHELSEA HOUSE
PUBLISHERS
An imprint of Infobase Publishing

Junior Drug Awareness: Steroids and Other Performance-Enhancing Drugs

Copyright © 2008 by Infobase Publishing

All rights reserved. No part of this book may be reproduced or utilized in any form or by any means, electronic or mechanical, including photocopying, recording, or by any information storage or retrieval systems, without permission in writing from the publisher. For information contact:

Chelsea House
An imprint of Infobase Publishing
132 West 31st Street
New York NY 10001

Library of Congress Cataloging-in-Publication Data

West, Krista.
  Steroids and other performance-enhancing drugs / Krista West.
      p. cm.—(Junior drug awareness)
  Includes bibliographical references and index.
  ISBN 978–0-7910–9748–9 (hardcover)
  1. Anabolic steroids—Juvenile literature. 2. Doping in sports—Juvenile literature.
I. Title. II. Series.
RC1230.W47 2009
362.29—dc22   2008014062

Chelsea House books are available at special discounts when purchased in bulk quantities for businesses, associations, institutions, or sales promotions. Please call our Special Sales Department in New York at (212) 967–8800 or (800) 322–8755.

You can find Chelsea House on the World Wide Web at http://www.chelseahouse.com

Text design by Erik Lindstrom
Cover design by Jooyoung An

Printed in the United States

Bang NMSG 10 9 8 7 6 5 4 3 2 1

This book is printed on acid-free paper.

All links and web addresses were checked and verified to be correct at the time of publication. Because of the dynamic nature of the web, some addresses and links may have changed since publication and may no longer be valid.

CONTENTS

Battling a Pandemic: A History of Drugs in the United States

When Johnny came marching home again after the Civil War, he probably wasn't marching in a very straight line. This is because Johnny, like 400,000 of his fellow drug-addled soldiers, was addicted to morphine. With the advent of morphine and the invention of the hypodermic needle, drug addiction became a prominent problem during the nineteenth century. It was the first time such widespread drug dependence was documented in history.

Things didn't get much better in the later decades of the nineteenth century. Cocaine and opiates were used as over-the-counter "medicines." Of course, the most famous was Coca-Cola, which actually did contain cocaine in its early days.

After the turn of the twentieth century, drug abuse was spiraling out of control, and the United States government stepped in with the first regulatory controls. In 1906, the Pure Food and Drug Act became a law. It required the labeling of product ingredients. Next came the Harrison Narcotics Tax Act of 1914, which outlawed illegal importation or distribution of cocaine and opiates. During this time, neither the medical community nor the general population was aware of the principles of addiction.

After the passage of the Harrison Act, drug addiction was not a major issue in the United States until the 1960s, when drug abuse became a much bigger social problem. During this time, the federal government's drug enforcement agencies were found to be ineffective. Organizations often worked against one another, causing counterproductive effects. By 1973, things had gotten so bad that President Richard Nixon, by executive order, created the Drug Enforcement Administration (DEA), which became the lead agency in all federal narcotics investigations. It continues in that role to this day. The effectiveness of enforcement and the so-called "Drug War" are open to debate. Cocaine use has been reduced by 75% since its peak in 1985. However, its replacement might be methamphetamine (speed, crank, crystal), which is arguably more dangerous and is now plaguing the country. Also, illicit drugs tend to be cyclical, with various drugs, such as LSD, appearing, disappearing, and then reappearing again. It is probably closest to the truth to say that a war on drugs can never be won, just managed.

Fighting drugs involves a three-pronged battle. Enforcement is one prong. Education and prevention is the second. Treatment is the third.

Although pandemics of drug abuse have been with us for more than 150 years, education and prevention were not seriously considered until the 1970s. In 1982, former First Lady Betty Ford made drug treatment socially acceptable with the opening of the Betty Ford Center. This followed her own battle with addiction. Other treatment centers—including Hazelden, Fair Oaks, and Smithers (now called the Addiction Institute of New York)—added to the growing number of clinics, and soon detox facilities were in almost every city. The cost of a single day in one of these facilities is often more than $1,000, and the effectiveness of treatment centers is often debated. To this day, there is little regulation over who can practice counseling.

It soon became apparent that the most effective way to deal with the drug problem was prevention by education. By some estimates, the overall cost of drug abuse to society exceeds $250 billion per year; preventive education is certainly the most cost-effective way to deal with the problem. Drug education can save people from misery, pain, and ultimately even jail time or death. In the early 1980s, First Lady Nancy Reagan started the "Just Say No" program. Although many scoffed at the program, its promotion of total abstinence from drugs has been effective with many adolescents. In the late 1980s, drug education was not science-based, and people essentially were throwing mud at the wall to see what would stick. Motivations of all types spawned hundreds, if not thousands, of drug-education programs. Promoters of some programs used whatever political clout they could muster to get on various government agencies' lists of most effective programs. The bottom line, however, is that prevention is very difficult to quantify. It's difficult to prove that drug use would have occurred if it were not prevented from happening.

In 1983, the Los Angeles Unified School District, in conjunction with the Los Angeles Police Department, started what was considered at that time to be the gold standard of school-based drug education programs. The program was called Drug Abuse Resistance Education, otherwise known as D.A.R.E. The program called for specially trained police officers to deliver drug-education programs in schools. This was an era in which community-oriented policing was all the rage. The logic was that kids would give street credibility to a police officer who spoke to them about drugs. The popularity of the program was unprecedented. It spread all across the country and around the world. Ultimately, 80% of American school districts would utilize the program. Parents, police officers, and kids all loved it. Unexpectedly, a special bond was formed between the kids who took the program and the police officers who ran it. Even in adulthood, many kids remember the name of their D.A.R.E. officer.

By 1991, national drug use had been halved. In any other medical-oriented field, this figure would be astonishing. The number of people in the United States using drugs went from about 25 million in the early 1980s to 11 million in 1991. All three prongs of the battle against drugs vied for government dollars, with each prong claiming credit for the reduction in drug use. There is no doubt that each contributed to the decline in drug use, but most people agreed that preventing drug abuse before it started had proved to be the most effective strategy. The National Institute on Drug Abuse (NIDA), which was established in 1974, defines its mandate in this way: "NIDA's mission is to lead the Nation in bringing the power of science to bear on drug abuse and addiction." NIDA leaders were the experts in prevention and treatment, and they had enormous resources. In

1986, the nonprofit Partnership for a Drug-Free America was founded. The organization defined its mission as, "Putting to use all major media outlets, including TV, radio, print advertisements and the Internet, along with the pro bono work of the country's best advertising agencies." The Partnership for a Drug-Free America is responsible for the popular campaign that compared "your brain on drugs" to fried eggs.

The American drug problem was front-page news for years up until 1990–1991. Then the Gulf War took over the news, and drugs never again regained the headlines. Most likely, this lack of media coverage has led to some peaks and valleys in the number of people using drugs, but there has not been a return to anything near the high percentage of use recorded in 1985. According to the University of Michigan's 2006 "Monitoring the Future" study, which measured adolescent drug use, there were 840,000 fewer American kids using drugs in 2006 than in 2001. This represents a 23% reduction in drug use. With the exception of prescription drugs, drug use continues to decline.

In 2000, the Robert Wood Johnson Foundation recognized that the D.A.R.E. Program, with its tens of thousands of trained police officers, had the top state-of-the-art delivery system of drug education in the world. The foundation dedicated $15 million to develop a cutting-edge prevention curriculum to be delivered by D.A.R.E. The new D.A.R.E. program incorporates the latest in prevention and education, including high-tech, interactive, and decision-model-based approaches. D.A.R.E. officers are trained as "coaches" who support kids as they practice research-based refusal strategies in high-stakes peer-pressure environments. Through stunning magnetic resonance imaging (MRI) images, students get to see tangible proof of how various sub-stances diminish brain activity.

Will this program be the solution to the drug prob-lem in the United States? By itself, probably not. It is simply an integral part of a larger equation that every-one involved hopes will prevent kids from ever starting to use drugs. The equation also requires guidance in the home, without which no program can be effective.

Ronald J. Brogan
Regional Director
D.A.R.E. America

Not Just for the Pros

Steroids are human-made drugs that make muscles grow bigger and faster than normal. Steroids are often taken illegally to change and strengthen the body.

Yet, it's not just Major League Baseball players, track stars, and professional body builders who take steroids. Teenagers are tempted as well. Sometimes, there are tragic consequences.

THE TRAGEDY OF A TEEN USER

Taylor Hooton was a 17-year-old high school student in Plano, Texas. He was a tall, good-looking guy with many friends. He smiled a lot, said "please" and "sir," drove a pickup truck, and pitched for the school's baseball team. He seemed to have a bright future.

In late 2002 and early 2003, his parents began to notice changes in Taylor. He developed acne on his back and quickly gained about 30 pounds. Emotionally, he became aggressive, irritable, and dishonest.

At first, the Hootons thought Taylor was just working hard at the gym and perhaps getting stressed out about typical teenager things: baseball, girls, homework. Yet, Taylor kept becoming more difficult to be around.

Eventually, Taylor's behavior became so unpredictable that he started to see a psychiatrist for help. Taylor's parents were worried about him. He admitted to the psychiatrist that he was using steroids, but he never admitted his steroid use to his parents. And none of Taylor's friends or coaches said anything to Taylor's family about possible drug use. All the signs of steroid use and abuse were there—Taylor's parents just didn't know how to read them.

Then, in July 2003, something Taylor did on a family vacation to England changed everything: He stole a digital camera and a laptop computer. When the family got home, Taylor was grounded. After one day, he asked his mother to lighten the punishment. She said no. Taylor then went to his room and ended his own life. Taylor hanged himself from his bedroom doorway on July 15, 2003, just a month after he turned 17.

Taylor's death was ruled a suicide. His parents and doctor said the suicide was directly related to the emotional side effects and depression brought on by illegal steroid use. A loss of confidence and a sense of hopelessness are two common feelings often associated with steroid use.

Police searched Taylor's room after his death. They found vials of steroids, along with syringes and needles, in Taylor's room. Tests on Taylor's body found steroids in his system.

Sixteen-year-old Taylor Hooton of Plano, Texas, used steroids to "get bigger." The 6-foot-2-inch, 180-pound teen was not aware of the depression he would feel as a result of using the drug.

No one knows why Taylor started using steroids. According to the Taylor Hooton Foundation (THF) Web site, a friend who talked to Taylor about his steroid use before his death says that Taylor insisted, "I'm not doing it for baseball. I'm doing it for myself."

Taylor's baseball coaches said they didn't know he was using steroids. They also said they never encouraged Taylor or any other students to use steroids. However, according to Taylor's father, Don Hooton, one of Taylor's coaches once suggested that Taylor "get bigger," perhaps prompting the use of steroids by the young athlete.

Whatever the reason he began using steroids, Taylor quickly felt the drug's effects. "There is a checklist of symptoms [of steroid use], and he was showing almost all of them," says Don Hooton on the THF Web site. "We didn't know any better. We should have."

Taylor's family started the Taylor Hooton Foundation with the goal of eliminating steroids and other performance-enhancing drugs from the youth population. They want to educate people about steroid use, support more scientific research, and encourage drug testing in high schools.

Stories like Taylor's may be largely unknown to the general public, but they are not uncommon. Steroids are becoming a big problem for typical teenagers.

Professional athletes that use steroids often have the help of doctors. These doctors pay attention to out-of-control, steroid-induced symptoms and changes in the body. Yet, teenagers usually don't have this kind of help. There were no doctors looking out for changes in Taylor.

Currently, steroid tests often are not required for high school students playing sports. However, some states—including Florida, New Jersey, and Texas—have made laws that allow random steroid testing for teens.

Teen steroid use is a growing problem. It's not going away anytime soon. To learn the what, when, who, and why of steroid use, this book is a good place to start.

In 2004, Don Hooton *(shown with son Taylor)* formed a foundation in his son's honor with the help of his family and friends. The Taylor Hooton Foundation works to educate young people about the dangers of steroids.

WHAT ARE STEROIDS?

Steroids are human-made (synthetic) drugs modeled after the human hormone called testosterone. A hormone is a chemical messenger in the body, sort of like an e-mail message that passes information between body parts. When hormones are released, they tell the body to do something. Testosterone tells the body to grow muscle. Some human-made steroids tell the body to grow muscle, too.

The official name of these steroids is **anabolic androgenic steroids**. *Anabolic* means "muscle building." Steroids build muscle by increasing the body's ability to make protein. As protein is made, muscles get bigger. "Androgenic" refers to male physical characteristics (such as facial hair and a deep voice). Steroids are androgenic because they are forms of testosterone, which is the hormone that makes males look like males. Steroids produce more male physical characteristics in users.

STEROID TESTING FOR TEXAS TEENS

In 2007, Texas passed a law to begin testing some 25,000 high school student athletes for steroid use. At that time, this was the largest steroid testing program in the world.

The purpose of the law, says Lt. Gov. David Dewhurst, is to "deter young people from putting that poison in their bodies and save lives all across Texas." Teen athletes in all high school sports—from football to wrestling to tennis—may be tested at random. Athletes that test positive or refuse to be tested will likely be suspended from play.

With this law, Texas became the third state to require steroid testing in public high schools. Florida and New Jersey also require it.

Although testosterone often is considered a male hormone, both men and women make testosterone naturally. Males make about 20 to 30 times more than females do.

Adding anabolic androgenic steroids to the body is like adding more testosterone. It throws off the balance of hormones in the user's body.

WHEN ARE STEROIDS ILLEGAL?

To call all steroids "illegal drugs" is actually a bit misleading. Sometimes it is just not true. Some steroids are legal, and some are illegal. It depends on why a person is taking the steroids.

Synthetic steroids were originally created to mimic testosterone and treat specific medical conditions. Today, there are many different types of synthetic steroids—each created for a specific purpose. Some are prescribed to treat severe acne, for example. Other steroids are designed only to build muscle.

Steroids prescribed by a doctor to treat a medical condition are perfectly legal, if they are taken as directed. Steroids taken without a medical need or a doctor's prescription are illegal. They can be very harmful to the body.

WHO USES STEROIDS?

In the United States alone, about one million people use steroids illegally. That's enough people to fill about 14 football stadiums. And the users may not be who you think they are.

Decades ago, illegal steroid use was largely restricted to professional athletes. Today, however, steroid use has spread to other groups of people looking to improve their appearances and performances. These include models, actors, amateur athletes, and teenagers.

Two federally funded studies provide information about teenage steroid use in the United States. The studies are called "Monitoring the Future," conducted by researchers at the University of Michigan, and the "Youth Risk Behavior Surveillance" conducted by the U.S. Centers for Disease Control and Prevention.

In general, both studies show that teens use steroids much less often than they use other illegal drugs, such as marijuana and cocaine. Yet, steroid use is still a problem—especially among teenage boys.

In 2006, for example, according to the "Monitoring the Future" study, more than twice as many teen boys as girls used steroids. The research showed that 12th grade boys are the biggest users of illegal steroids

STEROIDS BY ANY OTHER NAME

Like many illegal drugs, steroids are not always called by their proper name. On the streets, where the drugs may be sold or purchased illegally, steroids are known by many other slang names. Here's a rundown on a few of the alternative names for steroids:

- Juice
- Gym candy
- Pumpers
- Roids
- Stackers
- Weight trainers

in high school, while 10th grade girls are the least likely users.

Each year, "Monitoring the Future" researchers survey drug use by American 8th, 10th, and 12th graders. They ask what drugs they use, how they get them, and what they think about the dangers. This study has been

TEEN STEROID USE IN THE UNITED STATES

Two national studies examine steroid use among teenagers in the United States: "Monitoring the Future" (MTF) and the "Youth Risk Behavior Surveillance" (YRBS). Each study reports their results as percentages of boys and girls using steroids in different grades. The results are compared in the table on the right.

The two studies agree on one point and disagree on another. The studies agree that about twice as many boys as girls report using steroids illegally at all grade levels. Yet, they disagree on the grade level of highest use; the MTF says 12th graders use steroids most often, while the YRBS says 10th graders use steroids most often. Clearly the studies tell us a lot about teen steroid use—but not the entire story.

No one knows exactly why the two studies have different results, but it likely has something to do with how and when the studies were conducted. Overall, MTF is a much bigger project and more widely distributed than the YRBS.

Both studies gather information on young adult drug use by handing out surveys to students during class. The going on since the 1970s, so researchers can see how teen drug use changes from year to year. In 2006, teen steroid use was slightly less common than in years past.

Results from the "Youth Risk Behavior Surveillance" study generally agree with the "Monitoring the Future" study results. The 2005 "Youth Risk Behavior

	8TH GRADERS		10TH GRADERS		12TH GRADERS	
	MTF	YRBS	MTF	YRBS	MTF	YRBS
Percent of boys using steroids	1.2%	No data	1.9%	5.2%	2.7%	4.2%
Percent of girls using steroids	0.6%	No data	0.5%	2.5%	0.7%	2.3%

surveys ask students about what drugs they use and how often they use them. Student responses are never required and are anonymous, so the researchers never know who gave specific responses in the survey.

In 2006, MTF researchers handed out nearly 50,000 questionnaires to students in 410 different schools across the country, and in 2005, the YRBS researchers surveyed about 14,000 students in 159 different schools. The different sizes of the projects could partially explain the different results. More research is needed.

Surveillance" study reported that 4% of high school students nationwide had used steroids illegally at least once in their lifetime. And again, steroid use was a bigger problem for boys than for girls at all grade levels in high school.

WHY ARE STEROIDS A PROBLEM?

Steroid use makes competitive sports unfair. Steroid use changes the appearance of the user. Steroid use can have permanent effects on the body. Still, all of these problems are minor compared to the bottom line: Steroid use can kill people.

Steroids are psychologically addictive. They have been linked with heart attacks and strokes—even in young people. In addition, steroids can cause liver tumors, **cancer**, yellow skin, high blood pressure, and high cholesterol.

In short, scientists know that long-term steroid use causes health problems, but they don't know exactly why. The science of steroids is still being uncovered.

The History
of Steroids

Doping is the practice of using nonfood substances to improve athletic performance. As long as humans have competed against one another, they have used doping techniques. Steroid use is simply one of the most recent—and most problematic—forms of doping. But the idea has been around for centuries.

Ancient civilizations in South America, for example, commonly harvested and chewed coca leaves (from which cocaine is derived) to make them stronger. Greek Olympians used herbal concoctions that they thought would give them more energy. In the 1900s, athletes ingested a compound called strychnine to make their muscles work faster. Today, strychnine is better known as rat poison.

Only recently did people realize that the human body naturally makes hormones that can be manipulated to

TIMELINE OF DOPING DISCOVERY

This timeline shows the history of manipulating strength through physical chemistry and the use of performance-enhancing drugs.

2000 B.C.	Mayan people chew coca leaves (from which cocaine is derived) to enhance physical strength and endurance.
1000 B.C.	Greek Olympians drink herb concoctions to get an extra boost during competition.
1500–1900	**Castration** becomes a common way of removing testosterone from the male human body to create a castrato, a male singing star with a high voice.
1889	French physiologist Charles Edouard Brown-Sequard announces the physical benefits of injections from dog and guinea pig testicles.
1896	Scientists report that muscular strength improves after injections of liquid extracted from bull testicles.
1905	British scientist Ernest Starling defines hormones as the function-controlling chemicals in the body.
1905–1930s	Scientists work to identify the hormone secreted by the male testes, believing it has great potential for medical use.
1912	Scientists report curing male sexual dysfunction by transplanting human and animal testicular material.
1930s	Amphetamines (prescription **stimulants**) are commonly used to enhance sports performance.
1935	Natural testosterone is first isolated from the male testes. Synthetic testosterone is made from cholesterol in the laboratory.
1940s	Doctors begin using steroids to treat burns, wounds, and breast cancer, and to help patients recover from surgery.
1941	First known use of anabolic steroids in sports occurs as steroids are given to a racehorse.

1945	The book *The Male Hormone* subtly promotes testosterone use for athletes.
1966	East German Olympic coaches begin administering steroids regularly to athletes.
1967	International Olympic Committee drafts rules against performance-enhancing drugs.
1972	International Olympic Committee begins a full-scale steroid testing program.
1988	The Anti-Drug Abuse Act makes steroid trading illegal.
1990	The Anabolic Steroids Control Act replaces the 1988 law. NFL starts random, year-round testing for steroids.
1998	Steroids are discovered in the locker of Major League Baseball's Mark McGwire. He admits to using them, but they are not banned by baseball at this time.
2001	Major League Baseball begins steroid testing in the minor leagues.
2003	Major League Baseball begins steroid survey testing at spring training camps. About 6% of players fail these tests, but they are not punished.
2004	Major League Baseball begins steroid testing with punishment for positive test results. The Anabolic Steroid Control Act makes hundreds of specific steroids illegal without a prescription.
2007	Major League Baseball star Barry Bonds becomes the record holder for the most career home runs, but his record is over shadowed by talk of steroid use.
2008	Major League Baseball pitcher Roger Clemens testifies in a congressional hearing before the House Committee on Oversight and Government Reform that he never used steroids or human growth hormone, directly contradicting testimony from his former trainer.

improve athletic performance. In the 1800s, scientists discovered the power and purpose of testosterone. By the 1930s, human-made testosterone was used as a medical drug. Steroids surfaced as performance-enhancing drugs in athletic competitions as early as the 1940s.

Today, steroid use is not only a concern among amateur and professional athletes, but also among young people interested in changing the way their bodies look. Doping and steroid use, it seems, are not going away anytime soon.

THE DISCOVERY OF TESTOSTERONE

Like many revelations of science, the exact details on the discovery of testosterone aren't entirely clear. Many scientists spent years experimenting before they identified and isolated the hormone. And it all started with some unfortunate animals.

The **testes** are part of the male reproductive system. For centuries, humans have known that removing a male animal's testes makes it less aggressive. The animal also loses its male characteristics. In male humans, for example, this means hair and muscle loss. In male chickens, as another example, this means the comb and wattle stop growing and the chickens lose the instinct to fight. Testes removal, or castration, commonly was used to tame animals. Yet, no one understood exactly why castration worked. They just knew that it did.

By the 1800s, scientists became curious enough to experiment further. German professor Arnold Berthold (1803–1861) wanted to know how the testes controlled male characteristics. Did they put chemicals into the bloodstream, or did they act directly on the body's nervous system?

To answer this question, he castrated four roosters and transplanted the testes into the abdomens of two of them. The roosters without transplants became less aggressive. Their combs and wattles shrank. The roosters with transplants didn't change. Berthold concluded that because the testes were no longer connected to the body's nervous system, they must be secreting something directly into the blood.

Scientists knew that the testes secreted some substance that controlled maleness. They did not, however, know what that substance was. Berthold died before he could do more experiments.

Next came Charles-Edouard Brown-Séquard (1817–1894), a French scientist. He was famous for first suggesting the existence of hormones. He also was famous for experimenting on himself. To understand digestion, for example, Brown-Séquard would swallow sponges tied to long strings. Then he would use the strings to pull up the sponges, and study his own stomach juices.

To understand the testes, Brown-Séquard injected himself with liquids extracted from dog and guinea pig testes. He said he felt more energetic, and that his body and mind seemed healthier. His experiments prompted scientists around the world to experiment with liquids extracted from the male testes. This ultimately led to the discovery of testosterone.

It's not clear who first discovered and named testosterone. Multiple scientists were working on the problem at the same time. By 1935, testosterone had been identified and named. Soon after its discovery, a human-made version of testosterone was created in a laboratory.

HUMAN-MADE TESTOSTERONE

Once testosterone was discovered and shown to have some sort of healing potential, drug companies became

As a biochemist and cowinner of the 1939 Nobel Prize for chemistry, Adolf Butenandt is well known for his work with sex hormones. His research on sex hormone structure helped lead to the synthesizing of cortisone and the development of birth control pills.

interested in creating a version of the hormone that could be manufactured and sold. Three teams of researchers, funded directly by drug companies, raced to create the first human-made testosterone in the laboratory.

Two of the research teams submitted papers for publication in August 1935, describing how to make synthetic testosterone from cholesterol. The leaders of these research teams, Leopold Ruzicka (1887–1976) and Adolf Butenandt (1903–1995), received and shared the Nobel Prize for chemistry in 1939 for the discovery.

Almost immediately, the new steroids were tested in humans to treat many different problems that are naturally controlled by hormones. Synthetic testosterone was used to treat hypogonadism in men. Men with this condition lose muscle, body hair, and sexual function because their bodies do not make enough testosterone.

By the 1940s, synthetic testosterone was used to treat many conditions, including depression, burns, battle wounds, breast cancer, and **arthritis**. The healing and muscle-building powers of testosterone were widely known. It didn't take long for testosterone's potential as a performance-enhancing drug to take center stage.

EARLY TESTOSTERONE TESTING AND TREATMENT

In the 1920s, it seems everyone was experimenting with testicular injections. The doctor at San Quentin prison in California, for example, took advantage of the prison's population to do a few experiments of his own.

In 1918, prison physician Leo Stanley began transplanting the testicles from recently executed prisoners into living inmates. When word spread that Stanley's operations increased sexual drive, his services were in demand. His transplants were requested by prisoners with symptoms of asthma, epilepsy, diabetes, tuberculosis, gangrene, and more.

In just a few years, Stanley reportedly performed hundreds of testicular transplant operations. When he ran out of human testicles, he started using testes from rams, deer, goats, and boars, with equally acceptable results.

The medical value of testosterone was established early; the performance-enhancing potential for sports came much later. Beginning in 1966, East German Olympic coaches started giving steroids to male and female athletes in all sports in preparation for the 1968 Olympics. They kept it a secret from the rest of the world, gradually increasing the dose of steroids each year.

By the 1976 Olympics, the female East German Olympians had become so masculine—in appearance

TAKING AWAY TESTOSTERONE

Once the function and value of testosterone was discovered, much energy was devoted to getting more testosterone into the human body. In some parts of the world, however, removing testosterone was the goal.

Between 1500 and 1900, castration was fairly common. In Italy alone, about 4,000 boys were castrated each year. The hope, in many cases, was to create a wealthy singing star.

A young boy, usually between 7 and 9 years old, would be drugged with opium and soaked in a hot bath. Then, either the testes or all of the male reproductive organs were removed. Most boys—about 8 of every 10—did not survive the operation. Still, highly ambitious parents were willing to take the risk, hoping to make their sons into famous singing stars.

In a castrated male, the vocal chords do not fully develop. So castrati had high voices, like those of young boys. At the same time, the lungs and muscles grew to adult size, giving the voice power and strength.

At the time, people understood what castration did to the male voice, but they did not understand what was and performance—that people started asking questions. The female swimmers, for example, were asked why their voices were so deep. Everyone suspected steroid use, but there were no tests that could be done at the time.

When East and West Germany were unified in 1989, classified documents revealed the details of the Olympic

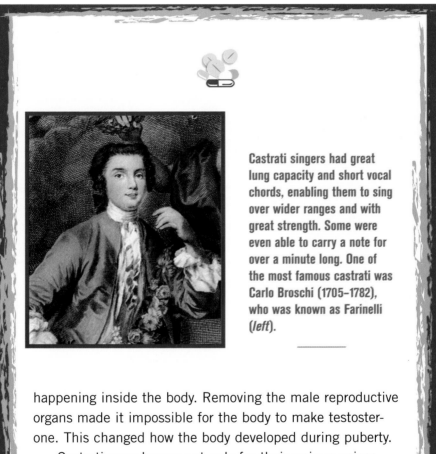

Castrati singers had great lung capacity and short vocal chords, enabling them to sing over wider ranges and with great strength. Some were even able to carry a note for over a minute long. One of the most famous castrati was Carlo Broschi (1705–1782), who was known as Farinelli (*left*).

happening inside the body. Removing the male reproductive organs made it impossible for the body to make testosterone. This changed how the body developed during puberty.

Castrati were known not only for their unique voices, but for their larger-than-life personalities. They were known for extravagant appearances, lavish lifestyles, and tantrums.

Former East German swimming stars *(from left)* Martina Gottschalt, Carola Beraktschjal, Jutta Gottscheid, and Karen Knoenig wait outside a Berlin courtroom in 2000 for the trial of Lothar Kipke. Kipke was accused of giving female members of the East German swimming team anabolic steroids, which were detrimental to their health.

athletes' steroid program. Today, many of those athletes are dealing with serious, long-term health problems. Between 500 and 2,000 former East German athletes are coping with liver tumors, heart disease, testicular and breast cancer, infertility, depression, and eating disorders.

The Science of Steroids

Chemically, synthetic steroids are almost exactly the same as natural testosterone. This is why they act like testosterone in the body. It is also why they are so difficult to detect when they are used illegally.

The only difference between natural testosterone and synthetic steroids is that a few atoms are attached to the synthetic testosterone molecule in different places. By chemically rearranging these detachable parts, scientists can create hundreds of different forms of steroids—making them difficult to detect in the body. Yet, they all do basically the same thing.

Like many illegal drugs, people can take steroids in different ways. No matter how they are taken, steroids do one thing once inside the body: They tell muscles to make more protein. And more protein means more muscle (and more hair, more fluids, more tumors, and more acne, for starters).

Steroid use comes with a long list of undesirable side effects. These have had a big enough impact on human health to prompt federal laws and legal action. The difficulty in controlling illegal steroids, however, is rooted in their chemistry.

STEROID CHEMISTRY

Natural testosterone and synthetic steroids have the same basic chemistry. Both are based on four connected rings of carbon atoms. A carbon atom is the smallest form of the element carbon. Carbon atoms often attach themselves, or bond, to other carbon atoms. They can form chains or rings.

Four six-sided carbon rings form the backbone of testosterone and synthetic steroids. Picture four stop signs stuck together top to bottom, with a carbon atom at every corner of each sign. Any carbon atom in this backbone can bond with other groups of elements. These other groups of elements are important in steroid chemistry.

In natural testosterone, the attached groups contain specific numbers of hydrogen and oxygen atoms. They are bonded to the carbon atoms in certain places. In synthetic steroids, the attached element groups also contain hydrogen and oxygen, but they can appear in different quantities and bond to different carbon atoms.

The chemical ingredients of testosterone include 19 atoms of carbon, 28 atoms of hydrogen, and 2 atoms of oxygen. Chemists write these ingredients as the chemical formula $C_{19}H_{28}O_2$. The chemical ingredients of a synthetic steroid are very close to this, but are not exactly the same. For example, tetrahydrogestrinone (THG), a popular synthetic steroid, has the chemical formula $C_{21}H_{28}O_2$. The two extra carbon atoms create a new chemical structure, but the steroid still acts like natural testosterone in the body.

For chemists, altering these chemical structures to create new steroids is fairly easy. They start with the basic testosterone molecule structure of four six-sided carbon rings. Then they make tiny changes to its ingredients and chemical arrangement. Voilà—a new synthetic steroid has been created.

HOW STEROIDS ENTER THE BODY

Steroids can enter the human body in different ways. Most commonly, athletes take steroids by mouth or inject them into muscles. They also can use skin creams, skin patches, or nasal sprays.

In many cases, users are stacking: taking two or more different steroids at once. They do this in hopes of getting bigger, faster. Some athletes practice pyramiding.

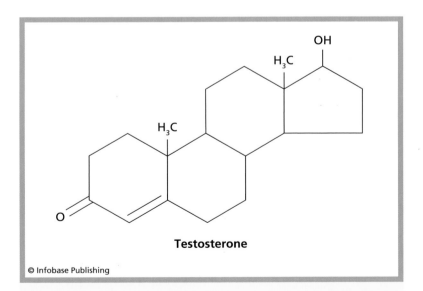

Testosterone

© Infobase Publishing

The image above shows the structure of testosterone, which is written as $C_{19} H_{28} O_2$.

They take steroids in 6- to 12-week cycles. They start with low doses, work up to higher doses, and end with low doses again. Neither stacking nor pyramiding has been proven as a more effective way to "get big."

Although a steroid dose can vary widely, many illegal steroid users take 10 to 100 times more than a legal dose.

DETECTING SYNTHETIC STEROIDS

Because it is fairly easy for scientists to make synthetic steroids, there are hundreds of different versions of steroids available to those who want them. Because there are so many kinds of steroids, it's hard to create tests that can detect all of them.

To find a specific molecule in the human body, chemists use a sample of bodily fluid (usually blood or urine). They analyze the chemical ingredients of the sample to see what molecules are present. Yet, in many cases, synthetic steroids break apart before they can be found this way.

By altering the method they use to analyze a sample, scientists usually can detect certain synthetic steroids before they break up. Still, they have to know what they are looking for before they find it. Because there are so many different versions of synthetic steroids, they can't always know ahead of time.

This constant searching for ever-changing molecules is commonly referred to as a game of cat and mouse. Scientists are the cats, constantly in search of new mice. The synthetic steroids are the mice, constantly on the move, quickly shifting positions, and outwitting the cat.

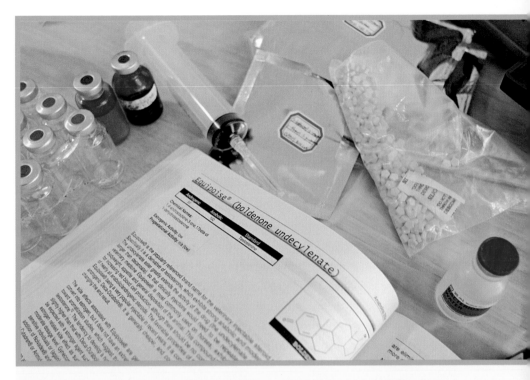

People learn to illegally create anabolic and androgenic steroids from gels and powders in their kitchens with directions from the Internet and privately printed materials. Pictured here are a steroid handbook and raw testosterone powder, among other tools.

HOW STEROIDS ACT IN THE BODY

Synthetic steroids act like hormones in the body. Whether ingested by mouth, inhaled through the nose, or secreted through the skin, steroids enter the blood and travel to muscles. When they are injected directly into muscles, they go straight to the action.

Muscles are made of cells. Inside each muscle cell are many receptor sites. Each site is a special place where hormones bind to the cell. Receptor sites are like locks, and hormones are like keys. Each receptor site is designed to bind a specific hormone.

STEROIDS AS CATTLE FOOD

Humans aren't the only mammals that use steroids to grow muscles. Cows grow bigger, and do it faster, by taking steroids. This makes more meat and more money for their owners when the cows are slaughtered for human consumption.

For decades, U.S. cattle have commonly been given the same performance-enhancing steroids that are illegally used by athletes. Growth hormones like testosterone are given to about 80% of the nation's beef cattle living on farms. Because their growth rate increases, these cattle can be sent to slaughter at a younger age. That improves profits for the owner.

The practice of giving steroids to cattle to increase profit has been banned throughout the European Union. It is still legal in the United States. Scientific studies suggest that steroid-enhanced meat could have harmful effects on humans who eat it, but the connection is not yet clear.

However, research has linked hormone residues in U.S. beef with high rates of breast and prostate cancer, as well as early puberty in girls. Other research has linked hormone use in cattle with smaller testes in male minnows living downstream of hormone-enhanced cattle lots. Research also has shown that female minnows exposed to synthetic hormones in a laboratory will develop male sex organs.

Eric Schlosser, author of *Fast Food Nation*, wrote a 2006 article on synthetic hormones and cows for *Sierra Magazine* called "Cheap Food Nation." In the article, Schlosser says, "U.S. fast-food and agribusiness companies aren't deliberately trying to mistreat animals, poison the land, or sicken their customers. But their relentless pursuit of the fast and the cheap is doing those very things."

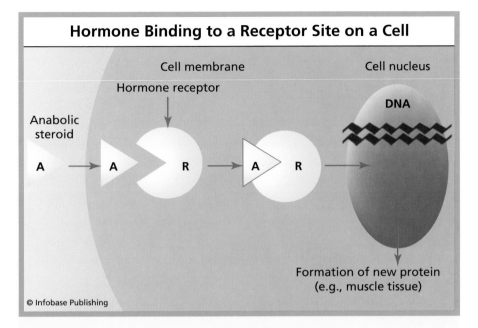

Hormone Binding to a Receptor Site on a Cell

Cell membrane

Cell nucleus

Hormone receptor

DNA

Anabolic
steroid

A

A   R   A   R

Formation of new protein
(e.g., muscle tissue)

© Infobase Publishing

This diagram illustrates the way in which a consumed steroid travels
into the nucleus of a cell, an act that signals DNA to form a particular
new protein—in this case, muscle tissue.

A synthetic steroid will bind to muscle cells at the
testosterone receptor sites. Once the steroid is bound,
the muscle cell starts to make proteins. The proteins
work to increase muscle mass and strength.

Scientists are still learning what synthetic steroids
might do. Steroids also could be bonding to other cells
in the body, such as **stem cells** (cells that are capable of
developing into many different types of cells). Or they
may interfere with the natural steroids produced by the
body: It's known that steroid users often stop making
natural testosterone.

Scientists do know that once a user stops taking steroids, he or she stops gaining muscle mass.

WHAT STEROIDS DO IN THE BODY

Steroids build muscle. That's why they are popular illegal drugs. But that's not all steroids do. Steroid use comes with a long list of side effects. Some are life threatening and some are related to how you look. Who gets what side effects depends largely on the user's age and sex, but anyone that uses steroids will experience some sort of change in the body.

BATTLING BODY IMAGE

The American battle with body image is not news to anyone—especially teenagers. In the minds of many people, women are supposed to be slim and beautiful and men are supposed to be strong and handsome. Media and the movies are filled with body images that are consistently svelte, yet largely unrealistic.

To help achieve the impossible body, some try steroids. Steroids make the body more masculine. This has some desirable physical effects for both men and women looking to change their appearances. In women, steroids reduce the percentage of body fat and increase muscle. For men, steroids usually mean more muscle mass.

Often, women see themselves as heavier than they really are. Diet pills, eating disorders, and even plastic surgery are some steps taken to change the physical body. Steroids not only reduce a woman's percentage of body fat, but also allow her to develop more defined muscles. (Never mind the extra body hair, facial hair, and deep voice.)

Less common, it seems, is the knowledge that men often see themselves as skinnier and weaker than they really are. Excessive exercise, combined with steroid use, is one way that men beef up their physical bodies.

A young person who takes steroids before or during puberty, for example, might harm his or her body's natural growing process. The artificial hormone levels trick the body into thinking it is done growing. Growth is stopped too early. This leaves the body short and underdeveloped for life. Or growth could be accelerated, forcing the body to mature before it is fully ready.

In the short term, it is difficult to deny that steroids work. Results can be seen quickly, depending on the dose and type of steroids taken. In fact, the results can be so rewarding that a user can become psychologically addicted to the drugs.

Yet, the consequences of long-term steroid use are real and irreversible. According to the Substance Abuse and Mental Health Services Administration (SAMHSA) and the National Institute on Drug Abuse, long-term health problems include:

- Heart attacks
- Strokes
- Liver tumors
- Cancer
- Jaundice (yellow skin and eyes)
- High blood pressure
- Increased LDL (bad) cholesterol levels
- Decreased HDL (good) cholesterol levels

If the body has a heart attack, it doesn't really matter what it looks like.

Irina Korzhanenko of Russia had to forfeit her Olympic gold medal for the women's shot put competition in 2004 after testing positive for the banned steroid stanozolol. Here, she throws the shot during the competition at the Ancient Stadium in Olympia, Greece—a sacred site where she had been the first woman to win a gold medal.

Because steroids are based on the male hormone testosterone, they produce some different side effects in men and women. In men, taking steroids slows or stops the natural production of testosterone. In women, taking steroids adds a male hormone that is usually only at very low levels. As a result, men get less masculine and women get more masculine.

Some side effects occur in both male and female steroid users, but others are specific to men or women. Note the following lists.

STEROID SIDE EFFECTS IN MEN AND WOMEN
- Tumors (non-cancerous)
- Cancer

- Jaundice (yellow skin and eyes)
- Fluid retention
- High blood pressure
- Increased bad cholesterol
- Decreased good cholesterol
- Strokes
- Severe acne
- Trembling
- Aggression

STEROID SIDE EFFECTS IN MEN
- Shrinking of the testicles
- Reduced sperm count
- Infertility
- Baldness
- Breast enlargement
- Prostate cancer
- Testosterone stopped

STEROID SIDE EFFECTS IN WOMEN
- Shrinking of the breasts
- Facial hair
- Male-pattern baldness
- Changes in menstrual cycle
- Clitoris enlargement
- Deepening voice
- Mood swings
- Depression

The long list of potentially harmful side effects is one reason that steroids are illegal. Yet, just because they are illegal doesn't mean they are easy to control. Like the science of steroids, the laws regulating steroids are constantly changing.

The Laws
of Steroids

The laws regulating synthetic steroids are different around the world. In general, laws in the United States are strict, and getting stricter. This is not the case in the rest of the world.

In many countries, it is legal to buy steroids without a prescription. But the rules vary. In England, for example, it is legal to possess steroids for personal use, but illegal to make them or supply them to other people.

In the United States, laws regulating illegal drugs first went on the books in the 1970s. These laws have been updated many times since then. Some of those updates have focused on controlling the illegal use of synthetic steroids. As forms of synthetic steroids change, the steroid laws change as well. Each new form of steroid technically requires a new law. The legal system has a hard time keeping up with the chemists who are creating new steroids.

Another problem is that to regulate illegal steroid use, law enforcement officials must know who is using steroids. To help find these steroid users, some states have started mandatory testing in high schools. Many professional sports organizations test athletes routinely. If such programs are successful, more states and organizations may enact similar testing laws in the future.

CONTROLLED SUBSTANCES ACT OF 1970

The Controlled Substances Act of 1970 governs the manufacturing, importation, possession, and distribution of many illegal drugs. The act includes five categories, or schedules, of drugs. Each schedule has its own criteria and requirements. The list of drugs governed by this act is extensive and has changed many times throughout history. The act categorizes drugs in the following groups:

- Schedule I drugs have no medical use (are not available by prescription). Heroin is a Schedule I drug.
- Schedule II drugs have medical uses, but are severely restricted. They can lead to serious physical dependence. Morphine is a Schedule II drug.
- Schedule III drugs have medical uses. Abuse can lead to low physical dependence. Steroids are Schedule III drugs.
- Schedule IV drugs have medical uses. Abuse can lead to limited physical dependence. Barbiturates and some stimulants are included here.
- Schedule V drugs have a medical use and low potential for abuse. Schedule V drugs include

cough suppressants with codeine and medications that contain small amounts of opium.

ANTI-DRUG ABUSE ACT OF 1988

The Anti-Drug Abuse Act of 1988 was the first major U.S. law to regulate steroids. The act made it illegal to

ARE STEROIDS REALLY ADDICTIVE?

There is still some discussion among scientists and politicians about whether steroids are addictive drugs. In practice, the exact definition may not be important. Legally, it is important to determine how addictive steroids are, because this affects how strict the punishments can be for illegally making, selling, or using them.

Addiction occurs when a person's body cannot function normally without a drug. Cocaine and heroin are examples of addictive, illegal drugs. They actually change the way the body functions; the body does not return to its predrug state.

Steroids are a little different. When a person is taking steroids, the drug changes the way the body works. Yet, when the person stops taking steroids, the body seems to return to normal. Men begin to produce testosterone again, and both men and women lose the extra muscle they gained while on the steroids. The body does not need the steroids to function normally.

Because of these reversible physical effects, some do not consider steroids to be addictive drugs. Still, most people believe that steroids are psychologically addictive.

possess steroids with the intent to sell or distribute them to other people.

In addition, the act changed the penalty for distribution of steroids from a misdemeanor (a criminal act punishable by a year or less in prison) to a felony (a serious criminal act punishable by more than a year in prison).

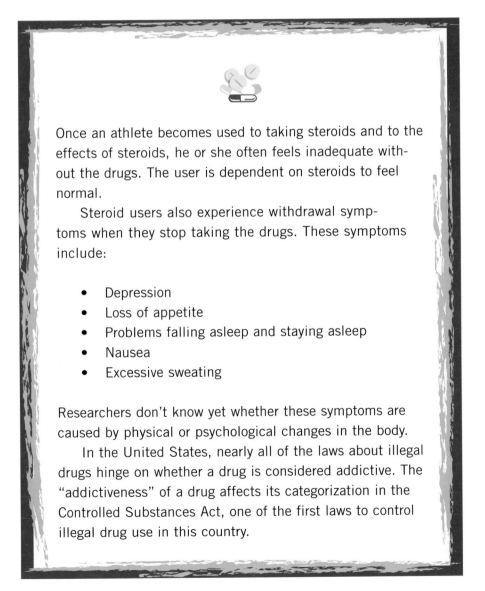

Once an athlete becomes used to taking steroids and to the effects of steroids, he or she often feels inadequate without the drugs. The user is dependent on steroids to feel normal.

Steroid users also experience withdrawal symptoms when they stop taking the drugs. These symptoms include:

- Depression
- Loss of appetite
- Problems falling asleep and staying asleep
- Nausea
- Excessive sweating

Researchers don't know yet whether these symptoms are caused by physical or psychological changes in the body.

In the United States, nearly all of the laws about illegal drugs hinge on whether a drug is considered addictive. The "addictiveness" of a drug affects its categorization in the Controlled Substances Act, one of the first laws to control illegal drug use in this country.

The act was in effect for two years before it was heavily revamped in 1990.

ANABOLIC STEROID CONTROL ACT OF 1990

The Anabolic Steroid Control act of 1990 officially established steroids as a group of drugs—with their own definition, rules, and regulations. The act originally listed 27

CHARLES E. YESALIS

Pick up nearly any book on anabolic androgenic steroids that was published since the 1990s, and Charles E. Yesalis will most likely be mentioned as an author or reference. Yesalis is a professor emeritus of Health Policy and Administration, Exercise and Sport Science, at The Pennsylvania State University, and one of the nation's leading experts on steroids and other performance-enhancing drugs. When lawmakers have a question about steroid use in the United States, they call Yesalis.

In the late 1980s, Yesalis directed the first national study on teen use of steroids. Later, he studied steroid use by weight lifters, college athletes, and professional football players. Since 1990, his studies show an increase in steroid use among teenagers.

Besides his own scientific discoveries regarding steroid use, Yesalis has consulted with lawmakers about steroid legislation. He has worked with the U.S. Office of National Drug Control Policy, the Drug Enforcement types of illegal steroids. It also outlined a relatively easy way to add more in the future.

The following questions must be answered for any drug regulated under the Anabolic Steroid Control Act:

- Is the drug chemically related to testosterone (look like the testosterone molecule)?

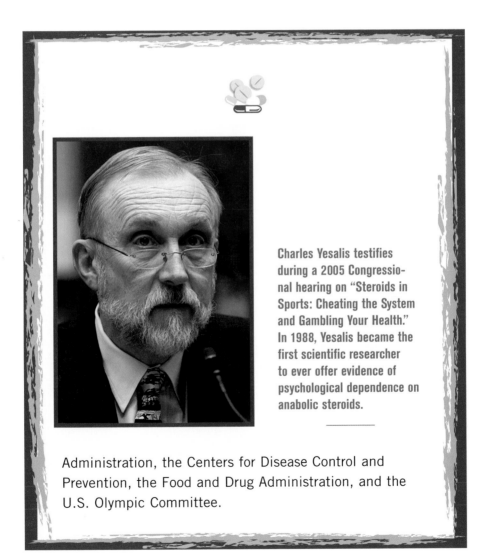

Charles Yesalis testifies during a 2005 Congressional hearing on "Steroids in Sports: Cheating the System and Gambling Your Health." In 1988, Yesalis became the first scientific researcher to ever offer evidence of psychological dependence on anabolic steroids.

Administration, the Centers for Disease Control and Prevention, the Food and Drug Administration, and the U.S. Olympic Committee.

- Is the drug pharmacologically related to testosterone (work like testosterone in the body)?
- Is the drug a type of estrogen, progestin, or corticosteroid (other types of hormones)?
- Does the drug promote muscle growth?

If the steroid fits these characteristics, it is considered illegal. The hard part is the last question. That's because it's difficult to show that a drug makes muscles grow. To answer this question, money must be found to fund a scientific study, the study must be planned and carried out, and then the results must be verified and published.

In many cases, the U.S. Drug Enforcement Administration (DEA) funds studies to determine whether a new synthetic steroid promotes muscle growth. Of course, it takes time and effort to answer this question.

By the time one steroid has been proven to grow muscle, officially making it illegal under this act, another steroid has been created and is in use. Because this new steroid has not yet been proven to build muscle, it is—technically—not yet illegal. This delay was a major concern for law enforcement.

ANABOLIC STEROID CONTROL ACT OF 2004

With the growing use of steroids in amateur and professional sports, by 2003 steroid laws had become a hot political topic. The Anabolic Steroid Control Act of 2004 did a lot of new things.

Perhaps most importantly, the act made the raw materials used to make steroids illegal, and increased the penalties for steroid users and dealers. At the same time, it eliminated the need for proof that a steroid increased muscle growth—a burdensome requirement of the 1990 act.

Former professional heavyweight boxer and steroid user Robert Hazelton lost both of his legs due to steroid abuse and became an advocate for adolescent steroid awareness. In this photo, he is shown testifying before Congress during a hearing on the Anabolic Steroid Control Act of 2004.

This law also brought political and media attention to the steroid problem in the United States. Many political leaders, including Senators John McCain (R-Arizona) and Joseph Biden (D-Delaware), testified in hearings about the dangers of the drugs. Former steroid users also testified.

Robert Hazleton, for example, was a boxer and steroid user. Hazleton told his story of steroid abuse, which ultimately led to the amputation of both of his legs and many medical problems.

STEROID LAW ENFORCEMENT

Steroid laws come from two places: federal and state governments. Federal law enforcement and penalties

OPERATION RAW DEAL

The largest federal crackdown on illegal steroid laboratories happened in September 2007. The Drug Enforcement Administration (DEA) arrested 124 people and took control of 56 laboratories in the project, called Operation Raw Deal.

For two years, the DEA had investigated the labs and the people involved. Ultimately, the agency seized 533 pounds (242 kg) of raw steroid powder, which originally came from China. According to the charges, dealers purchased the powder on the Internet and received instructions on how to convert it into useable drugs.

John Gilbride, the DEA officer in charge of Operation Raw Deal, said that to order raw steroid powder online, "All you need is a credit card and a place to deliver the steroids to."

Gilbride added that young people are most likely to purchase and learn how to use steroids online, but that individuals "from every walk of life" were arrested in the crack-down. This included firefighters, law enforcement officials, and people who just wanted to look healthier. No professional athletes were directly involved in this investigation.

come from the DEA. Yet, the states are free to make their own laws to control steroids as well.

At the national and international level, the DEA works to locate sources of steroids and laboratories that manufacture steroids in the United States. The DEA also enforces penalties for breaking the law.

Operation Raw Deal was part of the U.S. government's push to stop underground performance-enhancing drug buying and selling, and it is the largest case of government enforcement against steroids in U.S. history. Among other things, the investigation exposed a secret underground web of international drug dealers who prowled the Internet in search of young people wanting to buy steroids.

The first time a person is convicted of possessing illegal anabolic steroids, he or she receives a minimum fine of $1,000 and up to one year in prison. The first time a person is convicted of trafficking steroids, he or she is fined $250,000 and spends five years in prison.

For a second offense, the fine and prison time are doubled.

In most cases, the DEA works on a large scale to track down steroid sources. At the same time, state governments often work on a smaller scale to track down steroid users. Three states, for example, have enacted laws to test for steroid use among teens in public high schools.

In 2006, New Jersey was the first state to begin testing teenagers for steroid use. Governor Richard Codey, also a youth basketball coach, ordered the testing program in response to national statistics showing increased steroid use among high school students.

In 2007, Florida launched a one-year pilot program to test high school athletes for steroid use as well. Texas passed a law in 2007 that forced steroid testing of its 25,000 high school athletes, creating the largest steroid-testing program in the world.

Clearly, steroid use among amateur athletes—including teenagers in high school—is a growing concern for lawmakers and others. But many athletes at all levels face the decision of whether to use steroids to improve their performance.

5

Steroids in Amateur Sports and the Olympics

A s long as athletes have competed, they have searched for an edge over their competitors. The idea of using specialized equipment, instructions, or chemical substances is not at all new. Steroids are just one of the most modern methods of performance enhancement. And steroid use in amateur and Olympic sports can be particularly dangerous.

Amateur athletes are not paid to play. The levels of competition vary greatly. High school and college students playing sports on school teams are amateur athletes. So are most Olympians. What makes steroid use particularly dangerous for amateur athletes is the lack of supervision by a doctor.

Some Olympic athletes might have experienced coaches and doctors to help manage steroid use and abuse. Still, some amateur athletes are turning to steroids on their own. In many cases, they are not aware of the harmful side effects of steroid use—and are unable to see them when they appear.

This lack of supervision makes steroid use by amateur athletes particularly dangerous. Nevertheless, steroid use appears to be fairly common, particularly at the Olympics. Yet, it is difficult to know which has increased more: steroid use or the awareness of it.

TRENDS IN HIGH SCHOOL AND COLLEGE STEROID USE

It is safe to say that some high school and college students use illegal steroids to get stronger and look different. But studies show that the number of steroid users at this level has gone down slightly in recent years.

According to two nationwide studies of steroid use among high school students, the number of teenage steroid users is decreasing. The University of Michigan's "Monitoring the Future" study found that steroid use in 2006 was down slightly for 8th, 10th, and 12th graders. The Center for Disease Control's "Youth Risk Behavior Surveillance" study found a 2% decrease in teenage steroid users between 2003 and 2005.

At the same time, a five-year study by the National Collegiate Athletic Association (NCAA), released in 2006, found many fewer positive tests for steroid use among college athletes. There were 90 positive steroid tests in 1998–1999, 92 positive tests in 1999–2000, 46 positive steroid tests in 2003–2004, and 49 positive steroid tests in 2004–2005.

Officially, the NCAA outlawed steroid use in 1973, but the association did not begin testing for steroid use until 1986. Since 1989, the NCAA has conducted an

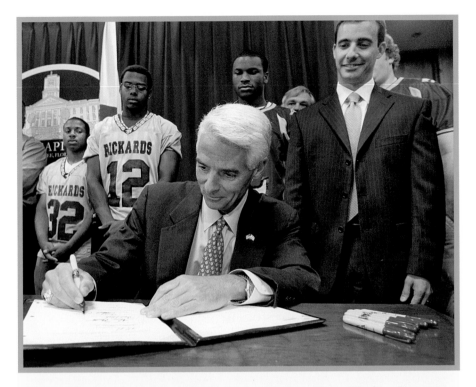

In an effort to prevent students from steroid abuse, Florida Governor Charlie Crist signed into law a bill in 2007 that established a pilot program calling for random drug testing of high school athletes participating in football, baseball, and weightlifting. Here, he signs the bill in the company of local high school athletes and Representative Marcelo Ilorente *(right)* of Miami. Llorente, who was a sponsor of the bill, noted that the plan was to focus on the sports in which greater muscle mass most enhances the performance.

anonymous survey every four years. In the 2001 survey, 57% of steroid users said they started taking steroids when they were in high school or younger. College competition, it seems, was not the only motivator.

Overall, the decrease in steroid use indicated by these studies may show that steroid education is working. Or they may show that steroids are simply harder to detect with mandatory testing methods.

EXAMPLES OF HIGH SCHOOL AND COLLEGE STEROID USE

Actual examples of high school and college athletes using steroids are difficult to come by. Many young athletes are using performance enhancers, but few legal systems or testing systems can identify them. For one thing, the tests are expensive; steroid tests can cost more than $100 per person.

As a result, not many high school or college steroid users are identified. Yet, this doesn't mean no one is using steroids. National studies say that fewer than 5 of every 100 high school students use steroids. Still, many researchers suspect the numbers are much larger.

One reason they believe this is that so many professional and Olympic athletes take steroids. And many have admitted that they started taking steroids in high school or college.

Football star Lyle Alzado said he started using steroids in college and never stopped. In high school, Alzado was an unimpressive football player. After he started taking steroids in college, he got noticed. His professional career began in the 1970s and lasted nearly two decades.

Alzado was known for his aggressive, combative style as a defensive lineman. At the height of his career, Alzado said he spent nearly $30,000 a year on steroids. At the age of 43, just seven years after retiring from football, Alzado died of brain cancer. Although there is no scientific link between cancer and steroids, Alzado openly blamed his cancer on his long-term steroid use.

Track star Marion Jones was suspected of drug use as early as high school. Back then, she missed a random

NFL star Lyle Alzado, pictured here in 1991 at his Los Angeles home, died of brain cancer in 1992. He believed the cancer was caused by his steroid use.

drug test for steroids and was successfully defended in court by lawyer to the stars, Johnnie Cochran. Jones eventually went on to win five Olympic medals. Yet, in 2007, she was forced to give them all back after finally admitting to using steroids.

Concerns over high school and college students using steroids have prompted many organizations to launch steroid education and testing programs. The National Federation of State High School Associations has a steroid awareness program entitled "Make the Right Choice." The NCAA tests athletes for steroid use year-round. And the Oregon Health & Science University offers steroid education programs to college athletic departments.

FIGHTING HIGH SCHOOL AND COLLEGE STEROID USE

Perhaps the most notable and widely used steroid education program comes from the Oregon Health & Science University (OHSU). OHSU has created two programs that help young athletes learn to avoid steroids and other performance-enhancing drugs. The programs are known as ATLAS and ATHENA.

The ATLAS (Athletes Training & Learning to Avoid Steroids) program has ten 45-minute sessions targeted to young male athletes. Coaches and athletes can obtain the materials and conduct the scripted sessions independently to educate other team members. The program is intended to help young athletes make healthy life choices. It has won multiple national awards. Details can be found at http://www.ohsu.edu/hpsm/atlas.cfm.

Likewise, the ATHENA (Athletes Targeting Healthy Exercise & Nutrition Alternatives) program has eight 45-minute sessions targeted to young female athletes. These team-administered sessions address the use of steroids to enhance sports performance. They also discuss eating disorders and other body-shaping drug use. ATHENA also has won multiple national awards. Details can be found at http://www.ohsu.edu/hpsm/athena.cfm.

Researched and created by OHSU's Health Promotion and Sports Medicine department, ATLAS and ATHENA are only one small part of the university's study of healthy lifestyles and sports performance. Learn about other areas of research at http://www.ohsu.edu/hpsm/.

HISTORY OF OLYMPIC STEROID USE

The international Olympic Games was one of the first places that the use of steroids became a public issue. At this level of competition, steroid use is much more than a small number of people making personal choices to enhance performance. It is an organized, often nationally sanctioned effort to drug athletes.

The first known, team-wide use of steroids by Olympic athletes occurred in 1952. That year, the Olympics were held in Helsinki, Finland. The Russian weightlifting team won seven medals and the coach reportedly confessed to giving his athletes steroids.

At this time, scientists weren't sure whether steroids could build muscle, and steroids were not technically illegal. By the 1960 Olympics, American weightlifters—along with many track and field athletes—also were using steroids.

The International Olympic Committee (IOC) organizes and oversees the Olympic Games. In 1967, the IOC banned the use of certain drugs, but steroids were not banned. It still wasn't clear whether steroids enhanced performance. Plus, no one knew how to test for them.

By 1972, the IOC was testing athletes for some performance-enhancing drugs. Still, there were no reliable tests for steroids. It took another 10 years to develop a test that could detect excess testosterone in the bloodstream. By this time, athletes were already using more advanced steroids. They left the body quickly, and these tests would not detect them.

Finally, in the early 1990s, the IOC started identifying some steroid users. Even then, the tests could not catch all steroid varieties. By this time, steroid use had spread to many Olympic sports, including swimming, cycling, wrestling, handball, and soccer.

EXAMPLES OF OLYMPIC STEROID USE

This section describes steroid use in a few Olympic sports. It doesn't include all the sports that have been affected by steroids. Yet, these examples made news around the world, and helped change the way people think about steroid use in the Olympics.

Swimming Steroid use in Olympic swimmers has made many news headlines. Starting in the 1960s, East German coaches gave steroids to all of their swimmers.

As a result, East German women dominated swimming for 30 years. At the first world swimming championship in 1973, East German women won 10 of the 14 gold medals available. Three years later at the Olympic Games in Montreal, they won 10 of the 12 gold medals in swimming. The IOC now knows that steroids helped the swimmers win medals. However, the committee usually does not take away Olympic medals unless the athletes admit to using performance-enhancing methods.

More recently, the Chinese swim team was caught using steroids. Before 1990, Chinese swimmers were not competitive in the Olympics. Then they won four gold medals at the 1992 Barcelona Olympics. Two years later, they won 12 of the 16 women's medals at the world championships. The quick success sparked suspicion. Since 1990, more than 40 Chinese swimmers have failed drug tests. That is three times as many failures in swimmers as any other country during the same period of time. Chinese swimmers have since dropped out of the spotlight.

Track and Field Steroid use in Olympic track and field athletes appears to be fairly common. As early as 1972, 68% of American track and field athletes admitted to using steroids. Since then, many track and field stars have been caught using steroids, or have admitted to steroid use.

Canadian sprinter Ben Johnson, for example, set a world record and won the gold medal in the 100-meter sprints at the 1988 Games in Seoul, Korea. Days later, his postrace urine tested positive for anabolic steroids. His medal was taken away. Although Johnson later admitted to taking steroids, he had successfully passed 19 previous drug tests.

In October 2007, American runner and jumper Marion Jones was stripped of the five Olympic medals—

THE WORLD ANTI-DOPING AGENCY

In 1999, the IOC created the World Anti-Doping Agency (WADA). The agency created the set of rules governing Olympic doping. It now helps to put those rules into action.

The doping rules are called the World Anti-Doping Code. At first, the Code was an attempt to standardize anti-doping policies from around the world. Today, it regulates doping, including steroid use, at the Olympics.

To enforce the Code's rule, WADA has testing agreements with 27 summer Olympic federations and 7 winter Olympic federations. Each federation is madeup of organizations that represent a sport in a country. The International Skating Union, for example, is a federation of figure skating organizations from 60 different countries around the world. WADA's testing agreements mean that all athletes associated with a federation can be tested for performance-enhancing drugs and other doping methods.

In 2006, WADA conducted more than 3,000 blood and urine tests on athletes from 72 different countries. WADA also helped test athletes before and during the 2006 Olympics in Turin, Italy.

In 2007, track star Marion Jones had tears in her eyes as she spoke to reporters after admitting in a federal courtroom that she used the steroid THG from September 2000 to July 2001. Jones pleaded guilty to lying to federal agents about drug use, as well as an unrelated fraud charge, and was sentenced to jail time.

three of them gold—that she won at the 2000 Games in Sydney, Australia. Jones admitted to taking steroids in 2000 and 2001, and lying about them in 2003. In early 2008, she was sentenced to a six-month jail term for lying about her steroid use. Jones claims her coach told her she was taking a nutritional supplement, and that later she realized it was a steroid known as "the clear."

Some people say that the widespread use of steroids in track and field makes it nearly impossible to compete without them. Charles Francis, Ben Johnson's former coach, says, "I don't call [steroids] cheating. My definition of cheating is doing something nobody else is doing." This attitude may be part of the reason that steroid use is so difficult to stop.

Weightlifting Steroid use among Olympic-level weightlifters began as early as the 1950s and continues today. Drug use is so common that entire teams often are banned from competition.

In recent Olympic Games, there has been a "three-strikes-and-out" rule. Under this rule, if three of a country's team members test positive for steroid use in one year, that country's entire Olympic weight lifting team is disqualified from competition. In 2000, the weightlifting teams from Romania and Bulgaria were banned from the Olympics under this rule. In 2004, at least eight weightlifters failed steroid tests and were banned from Olympic competition.

Steroid abuse by amateur weight lifters has been so troublesome that members of the International Olympic Committee have considered banning weightlifting from the Games until the problem can be better controlled.

Steroids in Professional Sports

Many professional sports are plagued by rumors of rampant steroid use. At this level of competition, steroids are big business.

In professional sports, athletes are paid to perform. And some are paid quite well. Steroid use by professional athletes is often more than just a personal decision to improve performance. It is an effort to keep one's job and perform for the good of a team. Rumors of team-approved and team-administered steroid treatments are not unheard of—but most are unproven. Fortunately, professional coaches and team doctors are usually aware of the side effects of steroid use.

This means that coaches or doctors can better identify professional athletes taking steroids and get them help, if help is desired. Still, it's unfortunate that some athletes think they have to take steroids to stay competitive and keep their jobs.

As the public becomes more aware of steroid use in professional sports, there is more pressure to keep it a secret. So professional athletes on steroids are always in need of newer, harder-to-detect steroids that also are better performance enhancers.

These harder-to-detect steroids make the drugs a pervasive problem. It seems everyone knows who is using steroids, but no one knows exactly what they are taking or how to test for it.

The responsibility of catching steroid cheaters falls to the organizations that oversee professional sports. Nearly all of these organizations have publicly banned performance enhancers, but few have been effective in actually stopping athletes from taking them.

PROFESSIONAL BANS ON STEROID USE

In the United States, just about every professional sports organization—including Major League Baseball, the National Basketball Association, the National Football League, and the National Hockey League—has banned the use of steroids and other performance enhancers. Often, steroids were banned not because they gave advantages to one athlete over another, but because of their dangerous side effects.

As a result, most organizations routinely and randomly test athletes for steroid use. They punish athletes who test positive, but the tests cannot keep up with the newest forms of steroids in use by athletes. The drugs always seem to be one step ahead of the drug testing methods. At the moment, catching steroid users seems to rely more on admissions from the athletes themselves.

PROFESSIONAL STEROID USE

There are no formal statistics on the number of professional athletes in the United States who use steroids. There are only personal stories. Yet, these stories, combined with readily observed changes in the performance of professional athletes over time, point to one unproven but unavoidable fact: Many professional athletes use steroids.

Nowhere is this steroid use more evident than in Major League Baseball. Many baseball players have admitted to steroid use and spoken about its widespread use in the sport. At the same time, long-standing baseball records have been broken recently and with seemingly little effort.

What follows are some examples of steroid use in baseball and other professional sports. These cases have changed the way the public thinks about steroid use and athletic performance in this country.

Major League Baseball

Two lines of evidence have made steroids a major issue for Major League Baseball (MLB): player admissions and shattered baseball records. Never mind what formal steroid testing has revealed about drug use by major league players; the players have said it for themselves. Among the most notable steroid admissions of the past decade:

- Pitcher David "Boomer" Wells said in 2003, "Twenty-five to 40% of all Major Leaguers are juiced (on steroids)."
- In his book, *Juiced*, outfielder Jose Canseco credits his entire career to steroid use and says that as many as 85% of players use steroids.
- Third basemen Ken Caminiti told *Sports Illustrated* in 2002 that he was using steroids when he won the 1996 Most Valuable Player award.

Former MLB star Jose Canseco discussed his own steroid use in his controversial 2005 memoir, *Juiced*. Released in a time when baseball was already undergoing investigations of steroid use among top players such as Barry Bonds and Jason Giambi, the book went on to name more players—including Mark McGwire—who Canseco claimed had also taken steroids.

- Pitcher Tom House told the *San Francisco Chronicle* in 2005 that steroid use was already widespread in professional baseball when he started his career in the late 1960s.

On top of such player admissions, some of baseball's longest-standing records—such as Roger Maris's record of 61 home runs in a single season—have been resoundingly shattered. Maris's record, set is 1961, stood untouched for more than 35 years. Then in 1998, the St. Louis Cardinals' Mark McGwire hit 70 home runs. The Chicago Cubs' Sammy Sosa finished the same season with 66 home runs. Then, in 2001, Barry Bonds beat them both.

Bonds hit 73 home runs that season while playing for the San Francisco Giants. As of the 2007 season, his record had not been broken. Bonds, McGwire, and many others have been under suspicion for steroid use.

In 1998, McGwire admitted using androstenedione, an over-the-counter supplement that turns into testosterone once it enters the body. The National Football League (NFL) and the National Collegiate Athletic Association (NCAA) had banned androstenedione. Yet, at that time, MLB had not banned the substance, so McGwire was not violating any rules. Still, his admission tainted his reputation.

MLB banned androstenedione in 2004. The next year, McGwire testified before Congress about steroids. Although he was asked repeatedly, McGwire never admitted to illegally using steroids as performance enhancers. He has never been convicted of steroid use.

Like McGwire, Barry Bonds has never fully admitted to steroid use or been convicted of breaking any laws. He has claimed that his trainers may have given him steroids without his knowledge. In late 2007, Bonds was accused of perjury—lying to federal courts under oath about using steroids.

The United States Congress, it seems, still wants to learn more about steroids and performance enhancers used in MLB. In 2008, MLB's star pitcher Roger Clemens

Star pitcher Roger Clemens *(right)* and his former personal trainer Brian McNamee *(left)* faced questions from Congress in 2008 during its hearing on "The Mitchell Report," regarding the illegal use of steroids and other performance-enhancing drugs in baseball. McNamee claims he had injected Clemens with steroids and human growth hormone; Clemens denies ever having taken them. Here, they are sworn in with attorney Charles Scheeler, a member of the investigating staff for former Sen. George Mitchell's report.

testified before the House Committee on Oversight and Government Reform that he never used steroids or human growth hormone, another performance enhancing drug.

The 2008 hearing began after Clemens's former trainer, Brian McNamee, said he injected the veteran with steroids and human growth hormone 16 times between 1998 and 2001, according to the *Washington*

Post's 2008 article, "On Capitol Hill, Clemens Denies Steroid Use." At the same time, Clemens's fellow pitcher and friend Andy Pettitte said the star admitted using human growth hormone in a private conversation.

Pettitte himself admitted to injecting himself with human growth hormone three times since 2002, and he has publicly apologized. The February 2008 congressional hearing ended without a resolution of any kind. Both Congress and MLB are deciding how to handle

THE BALCO SCANDAL

More than one high-profile athlete who has admitted to or been accused of steroid use has been connected with a company called BALCO. Athletes linked to BALCO include baseball's Barry Bonds and Jason Giambi, sprinters Marion Jones and Kelli White, and football's Bill Romanowski and Tyrone Wheatley.

BALCO stands for the Bay Area Laboratory Co-Operative. It's a California company that officially produced nutritional supplements. It turns out the company did much more than that. In 2003, federal investigators raided BALCO's offices and found records showing that the company had provided many athletes and coaches with steroids and other performance-enhancing drugs. BALCO's founder and three other men were arrested for drug trafficking.

Investigators learned that BALCO created and sold many different "designer" steroids—undetectable by the use of performance-enhancing drugs by professional athletes.

Bodybuilding

Steroid use is so pervasive in professional bodybuilding that many believe it is impossible to compete without using the drugs. Bodybuilding is a sport where competitors pose before judges and are rated for the aesthetic appearance of different muscle groups.

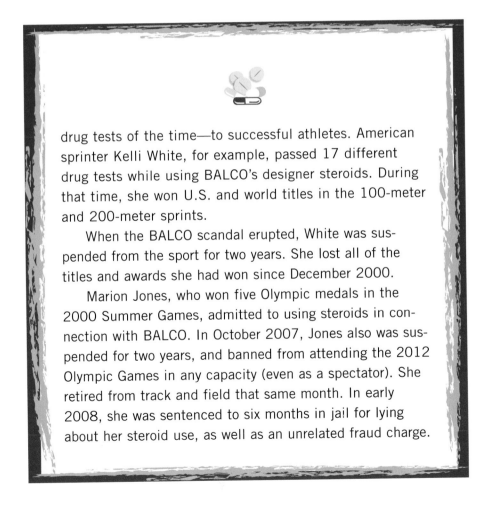

drug tests of the time—to successful athletes. American sprinter Kelli White, for example, passed 17 different drug tests while using BALCO's designer steroids. During that time, she won U.S. and world titles in the 100-meter and 200-meter sprints.

When the BALCO scandal erupted, White was suspended from the sport for two years. She lost all of the titles and awards she had won since December 2000.

Marion Jones, who won five Olympic medals in the 2000 Summer Games, admitted to using steroids in connection with BALCO. In October 2007, Jones also was suspended for two years, and banned from attending the 2012 Olympic Games in any capacity (even as a spectator). She retired from track and field that same month. In early 2008, she was sentenced to six months in jail for lying about her steroid use, as well as an unrelated fraud charge.

Arnold Schwarzenegger, movie actor and the current governor of California, is one of the most famous body-builders of all time. He has admitted to using steroids. Schwarzenegger's bodybuilding career began in the 1960s, when steroids were still legal. He has told many sources that steroids only helped him maintain muscle mass, but did not help him grow bigger. Schwarzenegger says he stopped using steroids in 1990 when they became illegal.

Cycling

Cyclists are legendary abusers of performance-enhancing drugs. The sport's largest road race, the Tour de France, is plagued by tales of steroid use. The Tour lasts 22 days and covers more than 1,800 miles (3,000 km) of wind-ing roads. In 1998, steroid use on the Tour made cycling history. A coach from the French team, Festina, was stopped during the race with a van full of illegal steroids and other doping equipment. A rider for Festina said that steroid use among Tour teams was common. At the same time, an official car for team TVM, of the Nether-lands, also was caught carrying illegal steroids.

When these discoveries were made public, other Tour teams refused to ride. Eventually, team TVM and four other teams withdrew from the race. Team Festina was disqualified.

According to Pat Lenahan, author of *Anabolic Steroids and Other Performance-Enhancing Drugs*, drug use has been part of the Tour since its inception in 1903. Cyclists have been known to boost themselves with such substances as caffeine, peppermint, cocaine, and brandy.

Football

The National Football League (NFL) was one of the first professional sports organizations to ban steroids. In 1987, the NFL banned the drugs and started testing

USING STEROIDS IN SECRET

Passing drug tests while using illegal steroids isn't too difficult. There are two reasons for this. First, there are more types of steroids than there are tests to detect those steroids. Second, athletes are smart.

There is an ongoing race between new steroids and new steroid tests. Manufacturers are always trying to develop new steroids to elude tests, and new tests are being developed to detect the steroids currently in use. But the tests are at least one step behind the steroids.

Also, athletes have many ways to elude steroid tests. These include:

- Taking masking agents that hide banned substances
- Using fluids to dilute steroids in the body
- Wearing condoms filled with clean urine samples
- Inserting other people's clean urine into their own bladders with catheters

More recently, freeze-dried urine has become popular in the United States. Users mix solid urine flakes with warm water to create a clean sample. As testing methods evolve, there's no doubt that more elaborate methods to beat the tests will evolve as well.

for them. The NFL's steroid policy is widely considered stricter and more effective than the policies of Major League Baseball and the National Hockey League.

The NFL conducts year-round, random drug tests for steroid use. If a player tests positive for steroid use, he is banned from play. After three positive tests, he is banned from the sport for one year. By 2005, more than 100 NFL players had tested positive for steroids, but none has ever tested positive a second time. Unlike professional baseball players, football players have largely managed to stay out of the media spotlight.

Hockey

The National Hockey League (NHL) officially banned the use of steroids in 2006. Yet, players argue that steroid use

STEROIDS COMMONLY USED IN PROFESSIONAL SPORTS

The list of steroids commonly used in professional sports is long and constantly changing. Here are some of the oldest, most common steroids used by the professional athletes of yesterday and today.

- *Anadrol*: Developed in 1960 as a prescription medicine to treat **osteoporosis** and anemia, anadrol is known as one of the strongest and fastest-acting steroids. It often is used by bodybuilders.
- *Dianabol*: This steroid was developed in 1958 by a doctor involved with the U.S. Olympic Weightlifting Team. It has fewer androgenic effects but still builds muscle mass.
- *Equipoise*: This steroid was developed as a treatment for racehorses. When used as a steroid, it

doesn't seem to be a big problem in the sport. Said Florida Panthers defenseman Eric Cairns, "You just can't be bulky and be a hockey player." The extra muscle mass can lead to more injuries, and can slow a player's skating.

Other performance-enhancing drugs, such as the stimulants Sudafed and Ripped Fuel, are more common problems in professional hockey.

Tennis

Professional tennis has banned steroid use and conducts drug tests. So far, none of the world's top tennis players has been convicted of steroid use. But the story

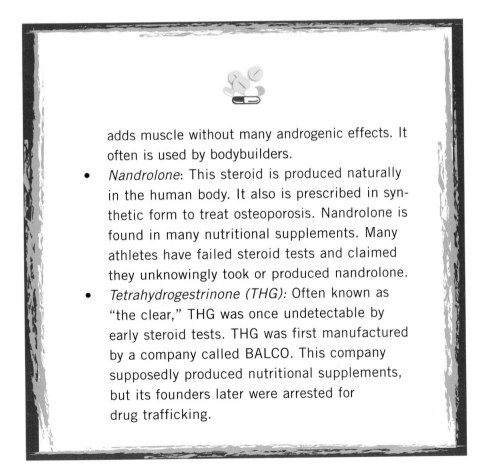

adds muscle without many androgenic effects. It often is used by bodybuilders.

- *Nandrolone*: This steroid is produced naturally in the human body. It also is prescribed in synthetic form to treat osteoporosis. Nandrolone is found in many nutritional supplements. Many athletes have failed steroid tests and claimed they unknowingly took or produced nandrolone.

- *Tetrahydrogestrinone (THG):* Often known as "the clear," THG was once undetectable by early steroid tests. THG was first manufactured by a company called BALCO. This company supposedly produced nutritional supplements, but its founders later were arrested for drug trafficking.

Tennis star Samantha Reeves is shown playing at Wimbledon's Tennis Championships in 2003. Reeves unknowingly ingested steroids in 1998 when she took a nutritional supplement that contained a variation of the illegal steroid nandrolone to help heal an injured ankle.

of the first female tennis player to test positive for steroids is memorable.

In 1998, teenage tennis star Samantha Reeves was enjoying her first year as a professional player when she failed a routine drug test for steroids. Reeves had been taking an over-the-counter nutritional supplement to help heal an injured ankle. The supplement contained Nor-André 19, a variation of the illegal steroid madrilène.

It seems that Reeves honestly did not know she was taking an illegal steroid. The International Tennis Federation believed her and did not punish her.

Legal Steroids

Steroids is a general term that refers to a big family of different chemical messengers, or hormones, in the human body. The human-made, muscle-building steroids are the ones that are often abused and taken illegally. They are formally called anabolic androgenic steroids. They mimic the hormone testosterone, and are taken both legally and illegally. But there is another group of steroids that has a different purpose and origin.

The corticosteroids are produced in the outer layer, or cortex, of the adrenal glands (which sit on top of our kidneys). These hormones influence how the body uses fat, sugar, and protein. They also help balance the salt and water content of the body. Taken legally as purified, high-dose medications, human-made corticosteroids can reduce inflammation.

Corticosteroids are widely prescribed as medications for many conditions, including asthma, arthritis, and itchy skin. Any health problem related to inflammation may be effectively treated with a corticosteroid.

LEGAL ANABOLIC ANDROGENIC STEROIDS

Anabolic androgenic steroids can act as medicines when their muscle-building effects are used to rebuild damaged bone or tissue in the human body. When prescribed by a doctor for a specific condition, steroids are legal. But countries have different ideas about prescription steroids.

For example, steroids are legally prescribed in the United States for anemia (low red blood cell count), as a muscle-building medicine to help patients recover from serious surgeries, and as testosterone replacement therapy for men with testicular cancer. But in Britain, prescription steroids are rare. This is because the British doctors' association suggests prescribing them only for anemia.

Nevertheless, anabolic androgenic steroids have been prescribed for a large list of medical conditions in the United States. Below is a snapshot of some of these conditions.

- *AIDS*. Acquired Immune Deficiency Syndrome (AIDS) occurs when the human immunodeficiency virus (HIV) attacks the body's immune system. People with AIDS cannot fight off illness. Over time, some grow weak and lose muscle mass. In these cases, anabolic androgenic steroids may be prescribed to help the person gain weight, feel stronger, and build muscle.

- *Anemia*. Anemia occurs when a person does not have enough red blood cells. These cells carry oxygen through the body. There are many causes of anemia. Some rare types of anemia can be treated with anabolic androgenic steroids. In immune hemolytic anemia, for example, the body destroys its own red blood cells. Steroid treatment can help stimulate the body to make more red blood cells to compensate for the loss.

- *Breast cancer*. Since the 1940s, certain types of breast cancer have been treated with anabolic androgenic steroids.

- *Burns*. Some anabolic androgenic steroids, mainly oxandrolone, are prescribed to treat severe burns. They help heal burn wounds and strengthen muscle mass.

- *Delayed puberty*. Puberty happens when a child's body changes into an adult's body that is capable of reproducing. Hormones fuel these changes, which usually start around age 12 or 13. Delayed puberty occurs when these changes happen later in life. Kids who experience delayed puberty usually catch up over time. But in some boys, the condition is treated with anabolic androgenic steroids. Temporary steroid treatment jump-starts puberty in these cases.

- *Osteoporosis*. There are two types of osteoporosis, a condition in which bones become less dense and can break easily. The most common type can be caused by a lack of calcium in a person's diet and poor hormone production in the body. In men, osteoporosis often is caused by low levels of testosterone. An anabolic androgenic steroid can be prescribed to treat this problem.

BIRTH CONTROL FOR BOYS

For decades, women have had the option of taking a birth control pill. The pill includes an extra dose of hormones that prevent the female body from releasing an egg. With no egg, the male sperm have no destination and fertilization does not take place. According to Planned Parenthood, more than 110 million women worldwide use the pill today.

In theory, there could be a birth control pill for men, too. So far, there is no such option. But it may be close.

Scientists at the University of Washington in Seattle are giving men an extra dose of human-made testosterone. This could trick the brain into thinking that the testes are producing enough sperm. If the brain thinks there is enough sperm, then it could stop sperm production.

According to the Seattle researchers, the extra testosterone could come in a daily pill taken orally, a patch or gel applied to the skin, an injection given every three months, or an implant placed under the skin once a year.

At the moment, availability of the male pill depends on whether the researchers can get enough funding to complete their work. Some men, it seems, are not eager to be on birth control. And if there is no market for the male pill, no one will pay for its development.

LEGAL CORTICOSTEROIDS

Corticosteroids can be given as medicines. Their main purpose is to reduce inflammation. Corticosteroids are available by prescription and as over-the-counter drugs.

Corticosteroids are not taken illegally as often as anabolic androgenic steroids are, but athletes still misuse them. They may be taken in large doses to mask inflammation caused by an injury, or they may be inhaled in smaller doses to open the airways and increase airflow to the lungs. If they are used for a long time without medical supervision, corticosteroids can be toxic and harmful.

Corticosteroids come as skin creams, inhaled medications, or pills. They also can be injected by a doctor. Some conditions treated with corticosteroids are outlined below.

Acne
In cases of severe acne, prescribed corticosteroid injections can help reduce inflammation. Large acne blemishes can burst and lead to scars. Injected corticosteroids will reduce inflammation and decrease the chances of scarring.

Arthritis
Inflammation and damage to joints in the body is known as arthritis. This condition can be treated with prescribed injections of corticosteroids. Most often, the corticosteroid prednisone is injected directly into the joints to reduce inflammation and relieve pain. In the short term, this treatment can make patients feel much better. But in the long run, side effects can make these injections undesirable. Side effects include weight gain, a temporarily rounder face, increased blood pressure, increased blood sugar, cataracts, and osteoporosis.

Asthma
Asthma occurs when a person's breathing tubes become inflamed and constricted. It can cause coughing,

IS AGING A DISEASE?

For many people, getting older brings a new collection of health issues to watch for, including decreased energy, loss of memory, and weakened bones and joints. Most of these age-related issues have proper names and official medical treatments. But the underlying cause is the same: The body is simply getting older.

As a result, some scientists have wondered if aging itself should be considered a disease. In a 1995 article in *Scientific American,* called "The History of Synthetic Testosterone," the authors discuss aging as a disease. If aging were recognized as a disease, it could be legally treated with anabolic androgenic steroids even before many common health issues present themselves. Some doctors, even today, prescribe steroids to middle-aged men to make them feel stronger and better.

Steroid therapy for aging men is common, say the authors, and gaining national scientific attention. In 1992, the National Institutes of Health (NIH) was willing to fund research on using testosterone therapy to treat physical problems and depression in aging men. The results were not definitive. And the debate over the value of testosterone therapy continues today.

The side effects of **menopause** in women, the natural end of a woman's reproductive cycle when menstruation stops, is sometimes treated with hormone replacement therapy. These *Scientific American* authors and others say that "male menopause," the point in life when males naturally start making less testosterone, could be treated in a similar way. But research continues on the value of such testosterone therapy.

wheezing, or shortness of breath. Asthma is commonly treated with prescription corticosteroids. An inhaler administers corticosteroids directly into the lungs. With this method, the drugs never enter the bloodstream. This reduces the chances that the drug will cause side effects. Patients with severe asthma may take cortico-steroids as pills or liquids. These medications work very well, but can have side effects if they are used for a long time. These side effects are the same as those that occur in people who take corticosteroids for arthritis. They include cancer and psoriasis. Corticosteroids are some-times used to treat inflammation and pain in cancer patients. They also are used to treat some types of blood cancers. Psoriasis causes red, inflamed, patches of skin. Corticosteroid creams are the most common treatment for this disease. In mild cases, corticosteroids can be pur-chased over the counter in cortisone creams. Stronger corticosteroid creams are prescribed by a doctor. They often are used in combination with other medications to treat severe cases of psoriasis and other skin problems, such as eczema.

8

Other Methods of Performance Enhancement

Getting an edge on the competition is not a new goal for athletes looking to win. In 1000 B.C., at the very first Olympics in Greece, athletes drank herbal concoctions to get an extra boost. The use of such stimulants continues today.

There are many ways to use non-food substances to improve athletic performance. Generally referred to as doping, these performance-enhancing methods are often physically invasive and difficult (if not impossible) to detect. What follows are some of the common, non-steroid, performance-enhancing drugs in use today.

BLOOD DOPING

Blood doping is the practice of artificially increasing the number of oxygen-carrying red blood cells in the body to enhance athletic performance. If the body's blood can carry more oxygen to the muscles, the athlete can perform better for longer periods of time. Blood doping is thought to be common in endurance sports, such as cycling and distance running.

In the past, blood doping literally meant injecting oneself with large quantities of red blood cells. The cells can be frozen, thawed, and injected. But these injections come with a risk of infection from diseased or damaged blood. In recent years, blood doping has taken on a different form.

The naturally produced hormone erythropoietin (EPO) stimulates the creation of red blood cells. In the 1980s, scientists figured out how to manufacture EPO. It was approved as a medical treatment for diseases such as anemia and cancer. Soon after, endurance athletes started using EPO to boost their performance. One injection of EPO under the skin can increase red blood cells in the body for as long as six weeks.

Professional cycling, perhaps more than any other sport, has been plagued by blood doping. In 2005, the World Anti-Doping Agency (WADA) reported that cycling had the highest percentage of positive tests for blood doping. Of 12,751 samples, about 4% tested positive. In the 2006 Tour de France, cycling's biggest event of the year, nearly 60 racers (including some top race contenders) were associated with a Spanish doctor involved in blood doping.

A blood test can identify EPO doping. Testing for the injection of extra red blood cells is more difficult. In the future, cycling may institute a "blood passport" program. Red blood cell counts and urine profiles would be taken repeatedly for each athlete. This would produce a profile of what is "normal" in each athlete's body. When an athlete is tested, results would be compared to

In 2005, seven-time Tour de France winner Lance Armstrong faced allegations of having taken EPO seven years earlier, based on tests of stored seven-year-old urine samples. He denied the allegations. Here, Armstrong *(left)* cycles as leader of the Discovery Channel cycling team during the Tour de France cycling race in 2005, along with Team T-Mobile leader Jan Ullrich of Germany *(center)* and Team CSC leader Ivan Basso of Italy *(right)*.

this passport to determine if the red blood cell levels are unnaturally high.

CREATINE

Creatine is naturally produced by the liver and stored in muscle. Its job is to release energy in muscles. It also gets rid of waste products in muscles, such as lactic acid, that are produced during exercise. These waste products can cause muscle pain and make muscles tired. Creatine can also be found in foods, such as meat and fish.

When taken as a performance-enhancing drug, creatine can produce small, short-term bursts of power and decrease fatigue. Such effects can benefit weightlifters and sprinters. They are of little use to endurance athletes.

At the present time, creatine is available in over-the-counter nutritional supplements and is not a banned substance for athletes. Side effects include weight gain and potential damage to the liver, kidneys, and heart.

GENE DOPING

Gene doping is the practice of using gene therapies to improve athletic performance. A gene is a piece inside a cell that regulates development or function in the body. When genes are inserted into cells to treat a disease, it is called gene therapy.

As a performance enhancer, gene doping could be used to insert a gene in the body that produces large amounts of hormones to build extra muscles, for example. Such a gene and the hormones it produced would be impossible to detect in blood or urine tests and could last for years in the body.

In 2006, the World Anti-Doping Agency banned the use of Repoxygen, a type of gene therapy. The product claims to make muscles release EPO when oxygen concentrations are low. When WADA banned Repoxygen, the therapy had not been extensively tested in humans. It is being developed to treat anemia (not enough red blood cells).

The use of Repoxygen was suspected, but not proven, in the 2006 Olympics in Turin, Italy. Experts suspect it will be a problem at future games as well. But so far there are no tests to detect gene doping. The World Anti-Doping Agency has asked scientists to work on the problem.

HUMAN GROWTH HORMONE

Human growth hormone (HGH), also known as somato-tropin and somatotrophin, is a naturally produced hormone that stimulates growth. HGH can make a person taller and stronger. The bones, organs, and muscles in the body grow and change permanently with HGH.

THE THOMAS HICKS STORY

After officials discovered that the first person to cross the finish line in the 1904 Olympic marathon had driven most of the race in a car, he was quickly disqualified. The gold medal was then awarded to American runner Thomas Hicks.

But under current race rules, Hicks would have been disqualified as well. Hicks used strychnine, a common performance-enhancing drug of the time. Today, the super-toxic strychnine is used as a pesticide to kill rodents. But taken in very small doses, strychnine makes the muscles of the body twitch, potentially improving an athlete's performance for a short period of time.

Hicks reportedly consumed 1/60 of a grain of strychnine and some brandy when he started to slow down during the race. The drug apparently gave him the energy to continue. But when he crossed the finish line, he collapsed. Hicks apparently took multiple doses of strychnine during the race. Experts suspected that one more dose of the drug would have killed him.

Hicks won the marathon and enjoyed athletic success. For obvious reasons, strychnine is banned as a performance-enhancing drug today.

Synthetic HGH was originally developed as a medical treatment for children whose growth was stunted. Prescribed as a medicine, it helped children build muscle and grow. HGH has also been used by athletes to increase performance.

American Thomas Hicks, shown among other 1904 Olympic marathoners, won the gold at the 1904 Olympic Games marathon in St. Louis, but he would have been disqualified under modern rules due to his use of strychnine. Researchers have theorized that the super-toxic drug most likely would have killed him had he taken just one more dose after the multiple doses he had taken during the race.

DON'T BE FOOLED ONLINE

"We are dedicated to serve those who wish to purchase steroids online. In our online shop there are only genuine products. All our products come directly from manufacturers and renowned legit pharmacies. . . . If you're looking for steroids that will effectively help you gain muscle mass, increase strength, and lose body fat, you are in the right place because we offer the fastest, low cost, and most reliable service on the internet! We deliver your anabolic steroids right to your front door step with a LOWEST PRICE promise!"

Sound like steroids are too good to be true? They are. But unfortunately, promises like this one are not uncommon online. This ad was discovered with a single keyword search, and there are many more just like it.

Many Web sites sell performance enhancement in a bottle. They are not hard to find. And their products do not cost much. Prices of "legitimate" steroids can run $10 and up. Their ease of use and low cost make them exceedingly dangerous.

There is simply no way to know if the products being purchased are the real thing. If a Web site is selling steroids without requiring a prescription, it is selling illegal drugs. Web sites that sell other pills and call them steroids are breaking the law, too. It is arguable which is more dangerous: taking a real steroid or taking a pill full of unidentifiable ingredients.

Either way, don't be fooled by fancy writing and false promises.

Historically, bodybuilders injected synthetic HGH along with steroids to increase body size and muscle size. There are currently no known tests that can successfully detect the use of HGH by athletes. Technically, HGH is a bodybuilding hormone but it is not considered a steroid. Steroids are chemically similar to testosterone. Synthetic HGH is similar to somatotropin.

INSULIN-LIKE GROWTH FACTOR

Insulin-like growth factor (IGF) is a hormone that affects almost every cell in the body. It also helps growth hormones (including HGH) do their jobs.

There is no scientific evidence that IGF enhances athletic performance. Still, some athletes take IGF along with HGH to try to build muscle mass and gain weight. Too much IGF in the body can cause swelling in the brain, coma, and enlargement of the heart.

IGF is currently banned by the World Anti-Doping Agency and other professional sports organizations, but there is no test to detect its use by athletes.

STIMULANTS

Stimulants are drugs that temporarily increase alertness and awareness in the body. They increase activity in the body's nervous system. In the long term, stimulant use is unlikely to help an athlete succeed. In the short term, it may help enhance performance.

As a result, some stimulants are banned from use in professional and amateur athletics. Cocaine and nicotine are examples of banned stimulants. Caffeine is a legal stimulant. For decades, stories of athletes using illegal stimulants to improve performance have surfaced in the press.

THE FOUNTAIN OF YOUTH

Marketers say that HGH and IGF can improve athletic performance. They also say these drugs can slow the effects of aging.

As one Web site explains, "HGH is believed to not only decrease the effects of the aging process, but also increase energy, mood, and lean muscle mass. It claims to improve sleep quality and sexual function and decrease negative cholesterol levels."

None of these claims is proven by science. The potentially deadly side effects are never mentioned; neither are the possible legal consequences of purchasing and using HGH for nonmedical purposes.

Many companies marketing nonprescription HGH promise results that are not backed by much science. And athletes are not the only targets.

In November 2007, for example, professional tennis player Martina Hingis tested positive multiple times for cocaine use, but denied using drugs of any kind. She then retired from the sport, avoiding the years-long legal process that might prove her innocence.

Shortly after Hingis's announcement, Dr. Gary Wadler of the World Anti-Doping Agency said, "The acute effects of cocaine probably, overall, would impair and not enhance performance. But within a two-hour window, you may actually have some enhancement—overcoming fatigue, reaction time, and so on."

Tennis players and other professional athletes are tested for stimulants in the body by taking a urine test. The tests can detect stimulants such as cocaine many days after they have been used, so they are not always accurate in predicting use as performance enhancers.

How to Quit Using Steroids

Steroids are unlike any other illegal drugs. Most drugs are abused for the desirable, temporary effects on users' minds. Steroids are abused for the desirable, temporary effects on users' bodies. But just as most mind-altering drugs wreak havoc on the body, most body-altering steroids also wreak havoc on the mind.

Strictly speaking, science has not yet proven that steroids are physically addictive. In theory, then, it should be relatively easy to quit using steroids because the body does not physically need them to function.

Yet, steroids are psychologically addictive. Users say that once they started taking steroids, they felt inadequate and weak without them. They wanted to continue using steroids, in spite of any side effects or professional consequences.

This psychological dependency, combined with whatever benefits steroid use brings, can make it difficult to quit using steroids. But it can be done. The physical effects are largely reversible (for better or worse). The mind just has to make the decision to quit.

If you think a friend is using steroids, there are some definite signs to look for. If some or all of the signs are there, don't let the issue go away. Look for help and work to stop steroid use and abuse. Steroid withdrawal may not be fun, but it will be temporary.

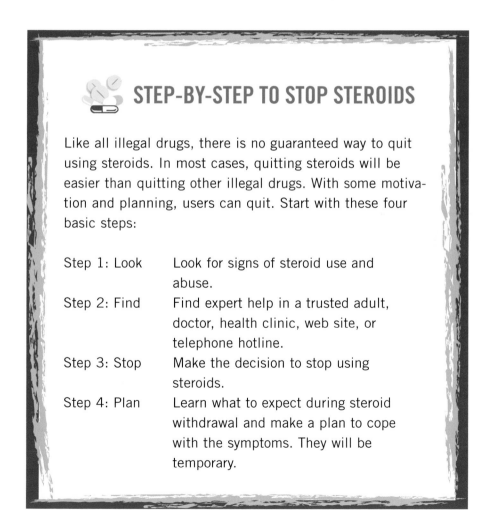

STEP-BY-STEP TO STOP STEROIDS

Like all illegal drugs, there is no guaranteed way to quit using steroids. In most cases, quitting steroids will be easier than quitting other illegal drugs. With some motivation and planning, users can quit. Start with these four basic steps:

Step 1: Look — Look for signs of steroid use and abuse.

Step 2: Find — Find expert help in a trusted adult, doctor, health clinic, web site, or telephone hotline.

Step 3: Stop — Make the decision to stop using steroids.

Step 4: Plan — Learn what to expect during steroid withdrawal and make a plan to cope with the symptoms. They will be temporary.

SIGNS TO LOOK FOR

According to the Substance Abuse and Mental Health Services Administration (SAMHSA), there are some ways you can tell if someone you know is using steroids. Look for these warning signs:

IN MEN:
- Baldness
- Development of breasts
- Impotence

IN WOMEN:
- Growth of facial hair
- Deepened voice
- Breast reduction

IN MEN AND WOMEN:
- Jaundice (yellowing of the skin and eyes)
- Swelling of feet or ankles
- Aching joints
- Bad breath
- Mood swings
- Nervousness
- Trembling

FIND HELP

The first place to turn for help is a familiar person: a parent, coach, teacher, friend, or other trusted adult. Tell the person why you are worried about your friend, and get a second opinion.

There might be other things going on in your friend's life. But if the person you talk with also believes steroid use might be happening, you may want look for professional help.

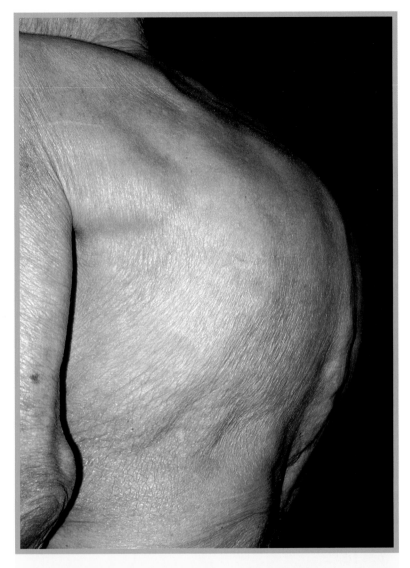

It is believed this elderly patient's collapsed spine—a sign of osteoporosis—is due to his use of prescribed steroids. Long-term steroid use also can hinder new bone formation.

First, ask your trusted adult to help make an appointment with a doctor and ask more questions. If you are not ready to talk to a doctor yourself, write down a list of questions and have the adult get the answers. Starter questions might include: Are there any steroid support groups in the area? Are there any local doctors with steroid expertise? Are there any clinics where steroid users can go to get support to quit? Gather as much information as possible about local steroids resources.

Second, do some homework. There is a lot of information about steroid use and addiction on the Web. The information on government Web sites that end in ".gov" can usually be trusted. Avoid information from Web sites that end in ".com." These are usually companies looking to make money.

Next, find someone to talk to. Many illegal drugs have drug-specific hotlines to call for help. There are multiple national hotlines to call to get help quitting cocaine, for example. But steroids are a little different. As of 2007, there are no known, steroid-specific, national hotlines. So finding someone to talk to can be a little harder when it comes to steroids, but it's not impossible. General drug abuse hotlines are one option to try.

Finally, use this knowledge to help the friend suspected of steroid use. Perhaps the information is simply passed along to him or her. Or the trusted adult uses the information to find help. The situation should help determine the actions taken.

STOP USE

Because steroids are not physically addictive drugs, they can be easier to quit than some other illegal drugs. But this doesn't mean quitting steroids is easy.

When people take steroids legally and then have to stop, they do what is called "tapering." This means they take lower and lower doses of the steroid over time. This gives the body a chance to get used to the changing steroid levels. When a person stops taking steroids altogether after tapering, the change from "some steroid" to "no steroid" is not jarring to the body.

As previously noted, steroids act like testosterone in the body. As a result, the human body may stop making its own testosterone over time. If steroid use is stopped

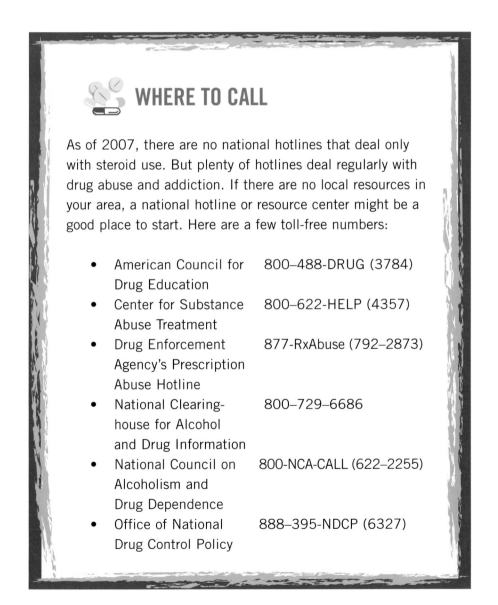

WHERE TO CALL

As of 2007, there are no national hotlines that deal only with steroid use. But plenty of hotlines deal regularly with drug abuse and addiction. If there are no local resources in your area, a national hotline or resource center might be a good place to start. Here are a few toll-free numbers:

- American Council for Drug Education — 800–488-DRUG (3784)
- Center for Substance Abuse Treatment — 800–622-HELP (4357)
- Drug Enforcement Agency's Prescription Abuse Hotline — 877-RxAbuse (792–2873)
- National Clearinghouse for Alcohol and Drug Information — 800–729–6686
- National Council on Alcoholism and Drug Dependence — 800-NCA-CALL (622–2255)
- Office of National Drug Control Policy — 888–395-NDCP (6327)

without tapering, the body has a hard time readjusting to the sudden drop in testosterone. But if steroid use is stopped gradually, the body has time to react.

It can take weeks or months for the body to return to normal after steroid use. Also, even when a person is tapering, he or she may still notice withdrawal symptoms.

MAKE A PLAN

Steroid withdrawal symptoms can be physical or emotional. Know what to expect when preparing to stop using steroids.

Physically, steroid withdrawal results in the loss of muscle and other features gained as a result of steroid use. In some cases, taking steroids can cause the body to stop producing its own testosterone. The brain thinks the body has enough testosterone, so no more is made.

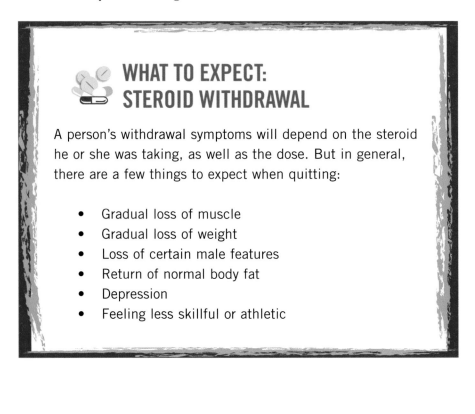

WHAT TO EXPECT: STEROID WITHDRAWAL

A person's withdrawal symptoms will depend on the steroid he or she was taking, as well as the dose. But in general, there are a few things to expect when quitting:

- Gradual loss of muscle
- Gradual loss of weight
- Loss of certain male features
- Return of normal body fat
- Depression
- Feeling less skillful or athletic

Then, if the steroids are suddenly withdrawn from the system, the body may be left entirely without testosterone. To give the body a chance to readjust its hormone production, steroids are best stopped by tapering.

Steroid withdrawal also can include psychological symptoms. Without steroids to improve appearance and performance, a user must learn to live with his or her own body. Some people become depressed and feel they are not good enough without the help of steroids. Some even become suicidal. Others go on with life largely unaffected by the whole experience. Science cannot yet explain or predict exactly what will happen emotionally during steroid withdrawal.

If needed, a person can get help with these symptoms from a doctor, trusted adult, or hotline.

STEROIDS CAN BE STOPPED: MAKE THE CHANGE

In the short term, steroids may seem like an easy way to get ahead. They can make a person look and feel stronger, and help him or her excel at sports.

Yet, in the long run, steroids can take a toll on the body and the mind. Physically, the list of side effects is long and undesirable. Emotionally, steroids can mess with the way a person sees himself or herself. And they can cause legal troubles for the user.

In the end, the "cons" of steroids far outweigh the "pros." As steroids tempt more teens, it can help to look beyond the quick fix. If someone is using steroids, work to stop the drug abuse and help make the change.

GLOSSARY

Addiction   When a person becomes physically dependent on a drug; when the body cannot function normally without the drug.

Anabolic androgenic steroids   Often just called "steroids." Anabolic means muscle-building; androgenic refers to male physical characteristics.

Anemia   A condition in which a person does not have enough red blood cells. These cells carry oxygen through the body.

Arthritis   Inflammation and damage to joints in the body.

Cancer   A disease in which some cells in the body grow faster than normal and destroy healthy organs and tissues.

Castration   The removal of the testes, or testicles, of a male animal.

Menopause   The natural end of a woman's reproductive cycle when menstruation stops.

Osteoporosis   A condition where bones become less dense and easily broken.

Stem cells   Cells that are capable of developing into many different types of cells.

Stimulants   Drugs that temporarily increase alertness and awareness in the body by increasing activity in the body's nervous system.

BIBLIOGRAPHY

Adams, Jacqueline. *Drug Education Library: Steroids*. New York: Lucent Books, 2006.

American Academy of Dermatology. "Prescription Medications for Treating Acne." *AAD* Web site. Available online. URL: http://www.skincarephysicians.com/acnenet/prescriptmeds.html.

Ashley, Steven. "Doping by Design." Scientific American Web Site. Available online. URL: http://www.sciam.com/article.cfm?SID=mail&articleID=0005AF2D-C69A-1FFD-869A83414B7F0000.

Associated Press. "Hingis claims innocence after positive test for cocaine." November 3, 2007. ESPN Web Site. Available online. URL: http://sports.espn.go.com/sports/tennis/news/story?id=3089841.

Bahrke, Michael S. and Charles E. Yesalis, editors. *Performance-Enhancing Substances in Sport and Exercise*. Champaign, Ill.: Human Kinetics, 2002.

Barbara, Philip. "Steroid buyers 'from every walk:' DEA agent." September 25, 2007. Reuters Web Site. Available online. URL: http://www.reuters.com/article/domesticNews/idUSN2429445520070925.

CBC Sports online. "10 Drug Scandals." January 9, 2003. CBC Sports Web Site. Available online. URL: http://www.cbc.ca/sports/indepth/drugs/stories/top10.html#6.

CBS/Associated Press. "Texas May Test for Steroids in High School." May 29, 2007. CBS News Web Site. Available online. URL: http://www.cbsnews.com/stories/2007/05/29/health/main2861011.shtml.

Coughlan, Sean. "Singing in the Pain." BBC News Magazine Web Site. Available online. URL: http://news.bbc.co.uk/2/hi/uk_news/magazine/4853432.stm.

Drug Enforcement Agency. "Anabolic Steroid Control Act of 2004." DEA Congressional Testimony March 16, 2004. DEA Web Site. Available online. URL: http://www.usdoj.gov/dea/pubs/cngrtest/ct031604.html.

Drug Enforcement Agency. "Steroids." DEA Web Site. Available online. URL: http://www.usdoj.gov/dea/concern/steroids.html.

Hoberman, John M. and Charles E. Yesalis. "The History of Synthetic Testosterone." *Scientific American.* 272 (1995): 76–82.

Janofsky, Michael. "Coaches Concede That Steroids Fueled East Germany's Success in Swimming." *The New York Times.* December 3, 1991. NYT Web Site. Available online. URL: http://query.nytimes.com/gst/fullpage.html?res=9D0CE1D A1731F930A35751C1A967958260.

Lenehan, Pat. *Anabolic Steroids and Other Performance-Enhancing Drugs.* New York: Taylor & Francis, 2003.

Matsumoto, Alan K., Joan Bathon, and Clifton O. Bingham III. "Rheumatoid Arthritis." The Johns Hopkins Arthritis Center. Available online. URL: http://www.hopkins-arthritis.org/arthritis-info/rheumatoid-arthritis/rheum_treat.html#cor.

Medicine Net. "Steroid Withdrawal." Medicine Net Web Site. Available online. URL: http://www.medicinenet.com/steroid_withdrawal/page2.htm.

"Monitoring the Future." *Overview of Key Findings 2006.* University of Michigan Web Site. Available online. URL: http://www.monitoringthefuture.org/pubs/monographs/overview2006.pdf.

National Collegiate Athletic Association. "NCAA Releases Five-Year Drug Test Report Indicating a Dramatic Decrease in Positive Steroid Tests." July 6, 2006. NCAA Web Site. Available online. URL: http://www2.ncaa.org/portal/media_and_events/press_room/2006/july/20060706_drugtestingreport_rls.html.

National Institute on Drug Abuse. "InfoFacts: Steroids." National Institute on Drug Abuse Web Site. Available online. URL: http://www.drugabuse.gov/PDF/Infofacts/Steroids07.pdf.

National Public Radio. "Texas to Test High School Athletes for Steroids. October 25, 2007. NPR Web Site. Available online. URL: http://www.npr.org/templates/story/story. php?storyId=15636588.

Patrick, Dick. "Until Now, Jones has been Steadfast in Doping Denials." *USAToday.* USAToday Web site. Available online. URL: http://www.usatoday.com/sports/ olympics/2007–10–05-jones-analysis_N.htm.

Puma, Mike. "Not the size of the god in the fight: Lyle Alzado biography" *ESPN Classic.* ESPN Web site. Available online. URL: http://espn.go.com/classic/biography/s/ Alzado_Lyle.html.

Schieszer, John. "Male birth control pill soon a reality." *MSNBC.* MSNBC Web site. Available online. URL: http:// www.msnbc.msn.com/id/3543478&&CM=EmailThis&CE=1.

Schlosser, Eric. "Cheap Food Nation." *Sierra Magazine.* Sierra Club Web Site. Available online. URL: http://www.sierra-club.org/sierra/200611/cheapfood.asp.

Shipley, Amy and Barry Syrluga. "On Capitol Hill, Clemens Denies Steroid Use." February 14, 2008. *Washington Post* Web Site. Available online. URL: http://www. washingtonpost.com/wp-dyn/content/story/2008/02/13/ ST2008021301149.html.

Society for Behavioral Neuroendocrinology. "Arnold A. Berthold." SBN Web Site. Available online. URL: http://www. sbn.org/purpose/founders.php.

Substance Abuse and Mental Health Services Administration. "Tips for Teens: The Truth About Steroids." SAMHSA's Alcohol and Drug Information Web Site. Available online. URL: http://download.ncadi.samhsa.gov/Prevline/pdfs/ phd726.pdf

The Ice Block Web site. Available online. URL: http://www. theiceblock.com/hockey/entry/steroids-and-the-nhl/.

The Steroids Working Group. "2006 Steroids Report." March 2006. United States Sentencing Commission Web site. Available online. URL: http://www.ussc.gov/USSCsteroidsreport-0306.pdf.

The Taylor Hooton Foundation Web Site. Available online. URL: http://www.taylorhooton.org.

USA Today. "New Jersey institutes statewide steroid-testing for high school athletes." October 16, 2006. USA Today Web Site. Available online. URL: http://www.usatoday.com/sports/preps/2006–06–07-nj-steroid-testing_x.htm.

"Youth Risk Behavior Surveillance." *Centers for Disease Control: Morbidity and Mortality Weekly Report.* 55 (June 9, 2006): 1, 16.

Yudt, Susan. "A Revolution in Birth Control." *Planned Parenthood.* Planned Parenthood Web Site. Available online. URL: http://www.plannedparenthood.org/news-articles-press/politics-policy-issues/birth-control-access-prevention/bc-revolution-6484.htm.

Zorpette, Glenn. "All Doped Up and Going for the Gold." *Scientific American.* 282 (2002): 20–22.

FURTHER READING

Adams, Jacqueline. *Drug Education Library: Steroids.* New York: Lucent Books, 2006.

Egendorf, Laura K. *Compact Research Series: Performance-Enhancing Drugs.* San Diego: Referencepoint Press, January 15, 2007.

Fainaru-Wada, Mark and Lance Williams. *Game of Shadows.* New York: Gotham Books, April 2006.

Gerdes, Louis I. *At Issue Series: Performance Enhancing Drugs.* Chicago: Greenhaven Press, November 2007.

Gruenwald Pfeifer, Kate. Amy B. Middleman (ed.). *American Medical Association Boy's Guide to Becoming a Teen.* San Francisco: Jossey-Bass, 2006.

Levert, Suzanne. *The Facts About Steroids.* New York: Benchmark Books, December 2004.

Monroe, Judy. *Steroids, Sports, and Body Image: The Risks of Performance-Enhancing Drugs.* Berkely Heights, New Jersey: Enslow Publishers, 2004.

Santella, Thomas M. *Body Enhancement Products.* New York: Chelsea House, 2005.

Stewart, Mark and Mike Kennedy. *Long Ball: The Legend And Lore of the Home Run.* Minneapolis: Millbrook Press, February 2006.

Walters, Eric. *Juice.* Victoria, B.C.: Orca Book Publishers, September 2006.

WEB SITES

ARE STEROIDS WORTH THE RISK?
TEENS HEALTH: NEMOURS FOUNDATION

http://www.kidshealth.org/teen/drug_alcohol/drugs/steroids.html

Articles and resources on steroid use by teens.

NIDA FOR TEENS: ANABOLIC STEROIDS
NATIONAL INSTITUTE ON DRUG ABUSE

http://teens.drugabuse.gov/facts/facts_ster1.asp

Basic steroid information for teens, including definitions, hormone information, and possible side effects on the teen body.

PERFORMANCE-ENHANCING DRUGS AND YOUR TEEN ATHLETE
MAYO CLINIC

http://www.mayoclinic.com/health/performance-enhancing-drugs/ SM00045

A site about steroids and other performance-enhancing drugs targeted to parents. If steroid use is suspected in a friend or family member, pass this site along. It may help.

TAYLOR HOOTON FOUNDATION

http://www.taylorhooton.org/

A foundation to fight steroid abuse amongst teenagers. The Web site tells the story of Taylor Hooton, a high school student from Texas who took his own life after abusing steroids.

PHOTO CREDITS

PAGE

14: Taylor Hooten Foundation
16: Taylor Hooten Foundation
28: Time & Life Pictures/ Getty Images
31: The Granger Collection, New York
32: AP Images
35: © Infobase Publishing
37: Mark Allen Johnson/ ZUMA/Corbis
39: © Infobase Publishing
42: George Tiedmann/ GT Images/Corbis
49: Newscom
51: AP Images
53: Courtesy of the Drug Enforcement Administration
57: AP Images
59: Neal Preston/CORBIS
64: Getty Images
69: Getty Images
71: AP Images
78: Newscom
88: AP Images
91: Popperfoto/ Getty Images
99: SPL/Photo Researchers, Inc.

INDEX

ABOUT THE AUTHORS

Understanding steroids involves understanding two basic things: competition in sports and the biology of the human body. **KRISTA WEST** has knowledge of both. She comes from a family of sports fanatics. When West is not writing or mothering her two boys, she loves to run, swim, and play outside. West has been writing about biology and physiology for young adults for nearly ten years. She holds a B.S. in zoology from the University of Washington and master's degrees in earth science and journalism from Columbia University. West lives in Fairbanks, Alaska.

Series introduction author **RONALD J. BROGAN** is the Bureau Chief for the New York City office of D.A.R.E. (Drug Abuse Resistance Education) America, where he trains and coordinates more than 100 New York City police officers in program-related activities. He also serves as a D.A.R.E. regional director for Oregon, Connecticut, Massachusetts, Maine, New Hampshire, New York, Rhode Island, and Vermont. In 1997, Brogan retired from the U.S. Drug Enforcement Administration (DEA), where he served as a special agent for 26 years. He holds bachelor's and master's degrees in criminal justice from the City University of New York.